Contents

MW00984151

Let's Go Camping! (Unit 1)...

   Spelling Skills: Long and Short *i; Spelling Theme Vocabulary; Visual Memory

   Reading Skills: Context Clues; Visual Discrimination; Words and Meanings

   Grammar & Punctuation Skills: Common and Proper Nouns; Capitalizing Proper Nouns

   Writing Skills: List; Postcard

Test Your Skills...12

At the Library (Unit 2).. 13

   Spelling Skills: Long and Short *e; Spelling Theme Vocabulary; Visual Memory

   Reading Skills: Auditory Discrimination; Context Clues

   Grammar & Punctuation Skills: Replacing Nouns with Pronouns

   Writing Skills: List; Personal Narrative

Test Your Skills... 22

Sports, Sports, Sports (Unit 3).. 23

   Spelling Skills: Compound Words; Spelling Theme Vocabulary; Visual Memory

   Reading Skills: Words and Meanings; Context Clues

   Grammar & Punctuation Skills: Identifying Subjects and Predicates

   Writing Skills: Opinion Paper; Sports Story

Test Your Skills... 32

Family Rap (Unit 4)... 33

   Spelling Skills: Contractions; Spelling Theme Vocabulary; Visual Memory

   Reading Skills: Context Clues

   Grammar & Punctuation Skills: Using Apostrophes to Make Contractions

   Writing Skills: Acrostic Poem; Personal Narrative

Test Your Skills... 42

Mystery Map (Unit 5)... 43

   Spelling Skills: Double Consonants; Spelling Theme Vocabulary; Visual Memory

   Reading Skills: Visual Discrimination; Visual Sequencing; Words and Meanings

   Grammar & Punctuation Skills: Using Capital Letters Correctly

   Writing Skills: Description; Directions

Test Your Skills... 52

Money Matters (Unit 6)... 53

   Spelling Skills: Schwa Sound; Spelling Theme Vocabulary; Visual Memory

   Reading Skills: Auditory Discrimination; Context Clues; Words and Meanings

   Grammar & Punctuation Skills: Kinds of Sentences—Question, Command, Exclamation, Statement

   Writing Skills: List; Creative Story

Test Your Skills... 62

Washington, D.C. (Unit 7)..63

    Spelling Skills: *ow* and *ou;* Spelling Theme Vocabulary; Visual Memory

    Reading Skills: Auditory Discrimination; Context Clues; Rhyming

    Grammar & Punctuation Skills: Using Capital Letters Correctly

    Writing Skills: Acrostic Poem; Journal Entry

Test Your Skills..72

In the Pond (Unit 8)...73

    Spelling Skills: Long *a* and Long *i;* Spelling Theme Vocabulary; Visual Memory

    Reading Skills: Auditory Discrimination

    Grammar & Punctuation Skills: Kinds of Adjectives

    Writing Skills: Creative Story; Information

Test Your Skills..82

Zoo Quiz (Unit 9)...83

    Spelling Skills: Suffixes *–ful, –er, –est, –less;* Spelling Theme Vocabulary; Visual Memory

    Reading Skills: Context Clues; Words and Meanings

    Grammar & Punctuation Skills: Using Comparative and Superlative Adjectives

    Writing Skills: Answering Questions; Description

Test Your Skills..92

Breakfast Is Served (Unit 10)...93

    Spelling Skills: *ea;* Spelling Theme Vocabulary; Visual Memory

    Reading Skills: Words and Meanings; Auditory Discrimination

    Grammar & Punctuation Skills: Action Verbs and Helping Verbs

    Writing Skills: Recipe; Personal Narrative

Test Your Skills..102

Once upon a Time (Unit 11)..103

    Spelling Skills: Homophones; Spelling Theme Vocabulary; Visual Memory

    Reading Skills: Synonyms and Antonyms; Visual Sequencing

    Grammar & Punctuation Skills: Capitalization

    Writing Skills: Fairy Tale; List; Complete Sentences

Test Your Skills..112

Postcard from Mexico (Unit 12)...113

    Spelling Skills: Compound Words; Spelling Theme Vocabulary; Visual Memory

    Reading Skills: Visual Sequencing

    Grammar & Punctuation Skills: Verb Tenses—Present, Past, and Future

    Writing Skills: Postcard; Descriptions; Complete Sentences

Test Your Skills..122

Record Form...123

Spelling Lists...125

Answer Key..133

Let's Go Camping!

My family likes to camp in the mountains every summer. We find a good spot near the lake to pitch our tent. That makes it easy to swim whenever we like. My brother and I look for firewood while Mom and Dad set up camp. Then we light a big fire. My family tells stories around the fire until we can't stay awake any longer. The next day, we pack a lunch. We get water to drink. We have a new boat this year. It's bigger than our old boat. We can't wait to put our boat in the lake. We'll sail over to Pine Island to go exploring. I wonder what we'll find?

Find It!

Read the spelling words.
Check off the words you can find in the story.

☐ pitch	☐ drink	☐ swim	☐ while	☐ light
☐ which	☐ find	☐ fire	☐ tent	☐ camp

How many spelling words did you find? _____

Spelling Practice

Read and Spell

Copy and Spell

Spell It Again!

1. pitch

2. drink

3. swim

4. which

5. light

6. while

7. find

8. fire

9. tent

10. camp

Find the Words

Write the missing spelling words to complete the sentences.

1. Let's _____ our _____ near the lake.

   which   tent   pitch

2. I can _____ _____ you fish for dinner.

   while   swim   tent

3. We will _____ the _____ to toast marshmallows.

   pitch   fire   light

4. Did you _____ a good place to _____?

   drink   find   camp

5. That _____, _____ is sweet, tastes good!

   which   tent   drink

Scrambled Words

Unscramble each word and write it on the line. Then match it to the correct spelling.

1. difn   **find**   tent

2. elwhi   _____   pitch

3. pihct   _____   light

4. ntet   _____   which

5. gthli   _____   drink

6. frei   _____   find

7. cpma   _____   swim

8. dirkn   _____   fire

9. chwih   _____   camp

10. wims   _____   while

Spell & Write • EMC 4539 • © Evan-Moor Corporation

Match the Meanings

Write the letter of the definition next to the spelling word.

_____ 1. find   a. during the time that something else is happening

_____ 2. while   b. a portable shelter held up by poles

_____ 3. pitch   c. to come across something

_____ 4. tent   d. to move through the water using the arms and legs

_____ 5. light   e. to put up a tent

_____ 6. fire   f. to swallow liquid

_____ 7. camp   g. flames, heat, and light produced by burning

_____ 8. drink   h. to live or stay outdoors

_____ 9. swim   i. to start something burning

_____ 10. which   j. a particular one

Skills:

Identifying
Proper and
Common
Nouns

Capitalizing
Proper Nouns

Naming Things

Nouns name a person, place, or thing.

- **Common nouns name any person, place, or thing.
  They do not begin with a capital letter.**

sister	doctor	deer

- **Proper nouns name a specific person, place, or thing.
  They begin with a capital letter.**

Idaho	Dr. Drake	Lake Tahoe

Cross out any letter that should be a capital letter. Then write the capital letter above it.

1. mount whitney

2. girl

3. forest ranger

4. mr. thompson

5. camp shasta

6. crystal lake

7. forest

8. brother

9. justin

10. pine tree

11. pine island

12. blue jay

13. montana

14. waterfall

Spellamadoodle

Write each spelling word on the outline of the drawing. You may use the words more than once. For fun, decorate the drawing.

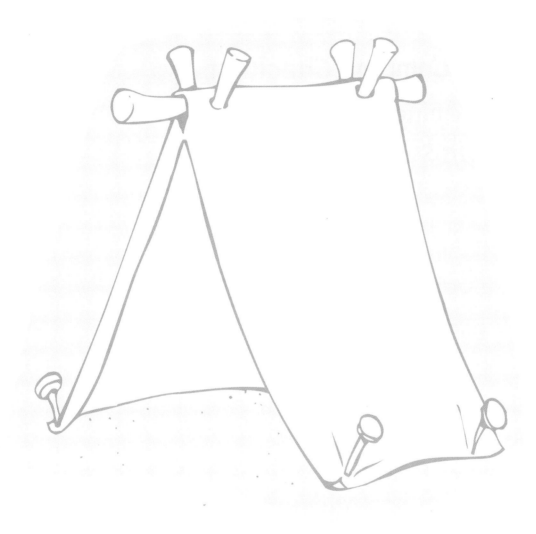

| light | tent | fire | pitch | swim |
| find | which | camp | while | drink |

What Should I Bring?

Pretend you are going camping with your family. There is a lake, hiking trails, and a lot of different animals. What will you bring? Make a list below.

My Camping Checklist

sleeping bag

swimsuit

Dear Friend . . .

You are on a camping trip with your family. Write a postcard to
a friend. Tell your friend all about the fun things you are doing!
Use as many spelling words as you can.

light	tent	fire	pitch	swim
find	which	camp	while	drink

To:

_____

_____

_____

✔ Check Your Writing

○ I used a capital letter for each name.

○ I checked my spelling.

Find the correct answer. Fill in the circle.

1. Which sentence has the correct capital letters?
   - ○ Ranger Moore showed us Rabbit Trail.
   - ○ My brother jake caught fish in Mirror lake.
   - ○ Camp Canoe is open all Summer long.

2. Which sentence has the correct capital letters?
   - ○ My Family hiked on Mt. red rock.
   - ○ We visited Red Rock Museum today.
   - ○ We saw many Deer at Breezy meadow.

3. Which word is spelled correctly?
   - ○ light
   - ○ lite
   - ○ lighte

4. Which word means "to discover or come across something"?
   - ○ pitch
   - ○ find
   - ○ which

Ask someone to test you on the spelling words.

1. _____

2. _____

3. _____

4. _____

5. _____

6. _____

7. _____

8. _____

9. _____

10. _____

5. Write the sentence correctly.

dad can let us swum wille he lites the fire

_____

_____

At the Library

The new library opened this weekend, and Dad took us to see it. There were many new things to see inside. I believe there are thousands of new books. The children's room is amazing! One bench has two friendly bears sitting on it. You can sit between the bears and read a book. There are

several computers, and someone is always there to help you. We took a tour and learned about the number system that keeps the books in order. It was easy for me to find my favorite author. We left after the tour, but Dad said we could go again next week.

Find It! Read the spelling words.
Check off the words you can find in the story.

| next | left | help | please | believe |
| many | between | order | author | title |

How many spelling words did you find? _____

Spelling Practice

Read and Spell	Copy and Spell	Spell It Again!
1. next	_____	_____
2. left	_____	_____
3. help	_____	_____
4. please	_____	_____
5. believe	_____	_____
6. many	_____	_____
7. between	_____	_____
8. order	_____	_____
9. author	_____	_____
10. title	_____	_____

Word Study

Read the words. Write them in the correct column. One word will be in both columns.

help	please	between	next
believe	left	many	

Sound of e as in eat	Sound of e as in bed
_____	_____
_____	_____
_____	_____
_____	_____

Circle the correctly spelled word in each row.

1. oredr   order   ordur

2. menny   manny   many

3. author   ather   awther

4. pleese   please   pleez

5. title   tiet   tittel

Spelling Words

Fill in the missing letters to make spelling words.

next	left	help	please	believe
many	between	order	author	title

1. pl ___ ___ se

2. l ___ ft

3. betw ___ ___ n

4. m ___ ny

5. n ___ xt

6. t ___ ___ le

7. ___ ___ der

8. h ___ lp

9. bel ___ ___ ve

10. ___ ___ thor

Picking Pronouns

> A **pronoun** is a word that takes the place of one or more nouns.
>
> Jenna works at the library.   She works at the library.

Use the pronouns below to replace the underlined words.
Write the pronouns on the line. You will use some pronouns more than once.

he   she   you   it   they   them

1. I believe <u>Tanya</u> checked out that book already. _____

2. You can find <u>books</u> on many shelves.   _____

3. Chad likes books about <u>dinosaurs</u>.   _____

4. <u>My mom</u> read aloud books to the children.   _____

5. <u>Children</u> can sit between the bears to read.   _____

6. Please help me look up titles on <u>the computer</u>. _____

7. <u>These books</u> are in a certain order.   _____

8. <u>Dad</u> left us in the children's room to read.   _____

Which Word?

Write the missing words on the lines.

1. Margie chose her book _____.

   believe   next   help

2. Trey is the _____ of this book.

   many   please   author

3. Can you read the _____ of this book?

   title   between   many

4. Dad will _____ us at the library.

   help   author   title

5. Jack sat _____ both bears on the bench.

   please   next   between

6. I found so _____ books at the new library.

   many   please   author

7. We _____ after the tour.

   order   left   please

8. I learned what _____ the books are in.

   please   left   order

Spellamadoodle

Write each spelling word on the outline of the drawing. You may use the words more than once. For fun, decorate the drawing.

| next | left | help | please | believe |
| many | between | order | author | title |

My Favorite Books

Do you visit the library often? What are some of the books you've read? List the titles of your three favorite books. Then write what each book was about.

My
3
Favorites

Title

1

Title

2

Title

3

Library Visit

Have you been to the library? What do you like to do there?
How do you find the books you want? Describe a trip to the library.
Use as many spelling words as you can.

next	left	help	please	believe
many	between	order	author	title

✔ Check Your Writing

○ I used a capital letter to begin each sentence.

○ I used a period to end each sentence.

○ I checked my spelling.

My Spelling Test

Find the correct answer. Fill in the circle.

1. Which pronoun would you use to replace the word **Maria**?

   ○ the
   ○ she
   ○ they

2. Which pronoun would you use to replace **the computer**?

   ○ she
   ○ they
   ○ it

3. Which word is spelled correctly?

   ○ many
   ○ meny
   ○ manny

4. Which word means "the writer of a book, play, or poem"?

   ○ title
   ○ author
   ○ order

Ask someone to test you on the spelling words.

1. _____

2. _____

3. _____

4. _____

5. _____

6. _____

7. _____

8. _____

9. _____

10. _____

5. Write the sentence correctly.

   we belleves this titel is nekst for our author

   _____

   _____

Sports, Sports, Sports

Everyone in my family likes to play sports. My mom is the coach of my softball team. We are called the Eastside Earthquakes. We won our city championship last season.

My big brother has a skateboard. He takes it to Irvine Skateboard Park to practice. Sometimes my friends and I go to watch.

When we finish our homework, my sister and I like to play basketball outside. My dad put up a hoop in the driveway. Sometimes he plays, too. Each time you throw the ball into the basket, you get a point. The first one to get twenty-one points wins.

Almost everybody I know is on some kind of sports team. Sports are not only fun, but also great exercise. What's your favorite sport?

Find It!

Read the spelling words.
Check off the words you can find in the story.

| point | coach | everybody | everyone | basketball |
| tie | outside | skateboard | earthquake | homework |

How many spelling words did you find? _____

Spelling Practice

Read and Spell	Copy and Spell	Spell It Again!
1. point	_____	_____
2. coach	_____	_____
3. tie	_____	_____
4. everybody	_____	_____
5. everyone	_____	_____
6. outside	_____	_____
7. basketball	_____	_____
8. skateboard	_____	_____
9. earthquake	_____	_____
10. homework	_____	_____

Two Words Make One

Draw a line between two words to make compound spelling words.

GO TEAM

basket   work

earth   ball

out   side

home   body

every   one

skate   quake

every   board

Skills:

Compound
Words

Spelling
Theme
Vocabulary

Mini-Crosswords

Complete the crossword puzzles using nine of the spelling words.

point	coach	tie	everybody	everyone
outside	basketball	skateboard	earthquake	homework

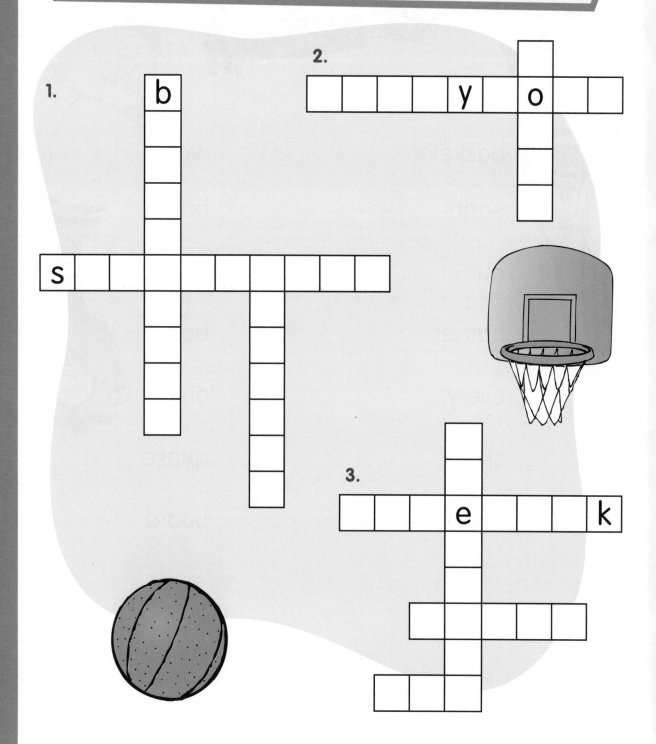

Which Part Is It?

> Every complete sentence has two parts.
> - A subject is the part that names the main person, place, or thing.
> - A predicate is the part that tells what the subject is or does.
>
> (My mom) bought me a basketball.

Circle the subject and underline the predicate.

1. My brother rides his skateboard at the park.

2. Our softball team won the championship.

3. Each player had several turns at bat.

4. Staci hit a home run in the sixth inning.

5. My whole family plays sports together.

Make a Match

Write the letter of the definition next to the word.

_____ 1. point

_____ 2. outside

_____ 3. coach

_____ 4. basketball

_____ 5. tie

_____ 6. skateboard

_____ 7. everyone/everybody

_____ 8. earthquake

_____ 9. homework

a. one who trains a sports team

b. sudden violent shaking of the earth

c. board with wheels that you stand on and ride

d. each and every person

e. unit for scoring in a game

f. schoolwork done at home

g. game played by 2 teams of 5 players each

h. when 2 teams have the same score

i. out of a building, or in the open air

Spellamadoodle

Write each spelling word on the outline of the drawing. You may use the words more than once. For fun, decorate the drawing.

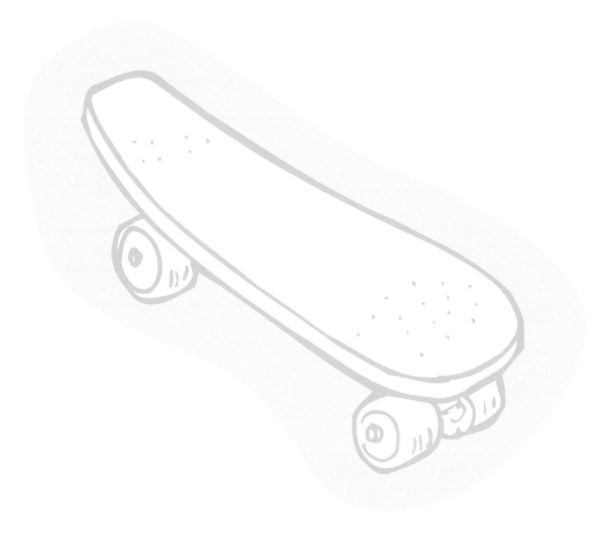

point	coach	tie	everybody	everyone
outside	basketball	skateboard	earthquake	homework

My Favorite Sport

What is your favorite sport? Do you like team sports like baseball?
Or do you like to play on your own, like tennis? Write about your
favorite sport below. Describe what you like about it.

_____

_____

_____

_____

_____

_____

_____

_____

_____

_____

_____

_____

_____

_____

The Great Game

Using your favorite sport, write about a great game. Write about what happened. Who were the teams? Who won? Tell about a game you actually saw or played, or make up a game. Use as many spelling words as you can.

| point | coach | tie | everybody | everyone |
| outside | basketball | skateboard | earthquake | homework |

✔ Check Your Writing

○ I used complete sentences.

○ I used correct spelling.

○ I used correct capitalization and punctuation.

TEST YOUR SKILLS — Sports, Sports, Sports

My Spelling Test

Find the correct answer. Fill in the circle.

1. In which sentence does the line separate the subject and the predicate?
   - ○ Torey's coach / took the team to the state finals.
   - ○ Torey's / coach took the team to the state finals.
   - ○ Torey's coach took / the team to the state finals.

2. In which sentence does the line separate the subject and predicate?
   - ○ Michael played / soccer last year.
   - ○ Michael / played soccer last year.
   - ○ Michael player soccer / last year.

3. Which word is spelled correctly?
   - ○ skatboarde
   - ○ skateborde
   - ○ skateboard

4. Which word means "a situation when two teams have the same score"?
   - ○ tie
   - ○ point
   - ○ river

Ask someone to test you on the spelling words.

1. _____
2. _____
3. _____
4. _____
5. _____
6. _____
7. _____
8. _____
9. _____
10. _____

5. Write the sentence correctly.

   our coche told evrybody to play bassketball outside

   _____

   _____

Spell & Write • EMC 4539 • © Evan-Moor Corporation

Family Rap

People who love you,
People who share,
They're the ones
Who'll always care.
A family.

People together,
People who say,
"We're proud of you
In every way."
A family.

People who help you,
People who make
A home that's happy.
It's no mistake.
A family.

People who know you,
People who see
All that you are,
And all you can be.
A family.

Find It! Read the spelling words.
Check off the words you can find in the story.

- [ ] I'm
- [ ] it's
- [ ] they're
- [ ] we're
- [ ] o'clock
- [ ] let's
- [ ] together
- [ ] home
- [ ] family
- [ ] that's

How many spelling words did you find? _____

Skills:

Contractions

Spelling
Theme
Vocabulary

Visual Memory

Spelling Practice

Read and Spell	Copy and Spell	Spell It Again!
1. I'm	_____	_____
2. it's	_____	_____
3. they're	_____	_____
4. we're	_____	_____
5. that's	_____	_____
6. o'clock	_____	_____
7. let's	_____	_____
8. together	_____	_____
9. home	_____	_____
10. family	_____	_____

Spell & Write • EMC 4539 • © Evan-Moor Corporation

Match and Spell

Draw a line between the two words that make each contraction.
Write the word on the line.

I'm	they're	we're	let's	it's	that's

let   is   _____

they   are   _____

that   is   _____

I   are   _____

we   us   _____

it   am   _____

Skills:

Contractions

Spelling
Theme
Vocabulary

Visual Memory

Spell It

Circle the correctly spelled word in each row.

1.	were'	we're	wee're
2.	hume	homme	home
3.	toogeter	together	tugethr
4.	let's	lett's	lets'
5.	family	fammile	famully
6.	thayre	they'er	they're
7.	oh'clock	o'clock	o'clocke
8.	tha'ts	thats'	that's
9.	I'm	I'am	I'me
10.	i'ts	its'	it's

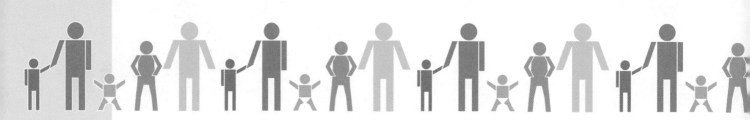

Spell & Write • EMC 4539 • © Evan-Moor Corporation

Contraction Action

▶ Use an apostrophe (') when making a contraction. The apostrophe takes the place of the missing letter or letters.

let us   let's   I am   I'm

Cross out the letter or letters in each set of words to make a contraction. Replace the letter or letters with an apostrophe. Write the contraction on the line. The first one has been done for you.

1. we   ~~will~~   __we'll__

2. have   not   _____

3. I   will   _____

4. they   are   _____

5. he   is   _____

6. it   is   _____

7. can   not   _____

8. did   not   _____

Circle It!

Circle the correct spelling.

1. Ime/**I'm** going to my soccer game.

2. My famile/**family** is coming to watch.

3. The game starts at four **o'clock**/oklock.

4. **It's**/Its going to be a good game.

5. Weer'e/**We're** going out for pizza afterward.

6. They know **that's**/that'ts my favorite food.

Spellamadoodle

Write each spelling word on the outline of the drawing. You may use the words more than once. For fun, decorate the drawing.

I'm	it's	they're	we're	o'clock
let's	together	home	family	that's

Families Care

Write a poem using the letters in the word family. Think of all the ways your family cares for you. Then write something that starts with each letter in the word. Your poem does <u>not</u> have to rhyme.

Examples:

Feeds and clothes me

Always there for me

F _____

A _____

M _____

I _____

L _____

Y _____

My Family Is Special

What makes your family special? Do you share a special tradition,
event, talent, or relative? Write about your family below. Use as
many spelling words as you can.

I'm	it's	they're	we're	o'clock
let's	together	home	family	that's

✔ **Check Your Writing**

○ I used a capital letter for each name.

○ I checked my spelling.

Family Rap

My Spelling Test

Find the correct answer. Fill in the circle.

1. Which contraction is made up of the two underlined words?

   Jenny <u>does not</u> want to leave her family.

   ○ don't
   ○ doesn't
   ○ didn't

2. Which contraction is made up of the two underlined words?

   Mando <u>is not</u> ready for his test.

   ○ won't
   ○ it's
   ○ isn't

3. Which word is spelled correctly?

   ○ familly
   ○ family
   ○ famly

4. Which word means "a place where you live or belong"?

   ○ home
   ○ o'clock
   ○ it's

Ask someone to test you on the spelling words.

1. _____
2. _____
3. _____
4. _____
5. _____
6. _____
7. _____
8. _____
9. _____
10. _____

5. Write the sentence correctly.

   letts get tugethr when theyre finished

   _____

   _____

 Spell & Write • EMC 4539 • © Evan-Moor Corporation

Mystery Map

I found an old map on the playground. The map shows a river. In the middle of the river are three islands. One of them looks different because it has a huge X on it. This is a mystery! I think it shows where a forgotten treasure is hidden. Maybe it's gold coins or jewels. Do you want to help me look for it? We need to find it before it disappears. Meet me at the tunnel near the playground. Bring your backpack with the zipper and a compass. We might have to carry something back. Get ready to solve the mystery!

Find It! Read the spelling words.
Check off the words you can find in the story.

letter	different	pattern	middle	zipper
carry	Mississippi	compass	backpack	river

How many spelling words did you find? _____

Spelling Practice

Read and Spell	Copy and Spell	Spell It Again!
1. letter	_____	_____
2. different	_____	_____
3. pattern	_____	_____
4. middle	_____	_____
5. Mississippi	_____	_____
6. zipper	_____	_____
7. carry	_____	_____
8. compass	_____	_____
9. backpack	_____	_____
10. river	_____	_____

Spell & Write • EMC 4539 • © Evan-Moor Corporation

Word Study

Fill in the missing double letters to make spelling words.

le ____ ____ er   pa ____ ____ ern

compa ____ ____   ca ____ ____ y

di ____ ____ erent   zi ____ ____ er

mi ____ ____ le   Mi ____ ____ issi ____ ____ i

Circle each spelling word.

compassrivermiddlelettercarryzipperbackpack

differentpatterncarrybackpackmiddleMississippi

letterMississippizipperrivercompasspatterndifferent

Skills:

Spelling Words
with Double
Consonants

Spelling
Theme
Vocabulary

Matching
Words
with Their
Meanings

Crossword Challenge

Complete the crossword puzzle using words from the spelling list.
You will not use one word.

| letter | different | pattern | middle | Mississippi |
| zipper | carry | compass | backpack | river |

Across

2. halfway between two things
5. a repeating arrangement of colors, shapes, and figures
7. to hold something and take it somewhere
8. a message that you write to someone
9. an instrument for finding directions

Down

1. a fastener for clothes or other objects
3. not the same
4. a large bag you carry on your back
6. a large natural stream of fresh water

Spell & Write • EMC 4539 • © Evan-Moor Corporation

Word Search

Find and circle each spelling word. Words can go across, down, or diagonally.

letter	different	pattern	middle	Mississippi
zipper	carry	compass	backpack	river

```
K T S S A P M O C I A N
C A N A I L Y O U Z U R
A K I E A R E O R I Z E
P E A R R O I T O P I T
K R E A K E I V T P A T
C L C A K E F L E E R A
A S K F O R I F O R R P
B M I S S I S S I P P I
S O M E W H M I D D L E
```

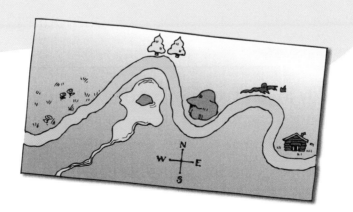

Capital Letters

Use a capital letter to begin:

• a sentence

> We found a map.

• days of the week, months of the year, and holidays

> Tuesday   October   Halloween

• names of specific persons, places, or things

> Jason   Alabama   Red Rock

Circle each word that needs a capital letter. Write the capitalized words on the lines.

1. i read a mystery about two kids named wyatt and dylan.

   _____

2. they were in hawaii looking for buried treasure.

   _____

3. all summer, their friend jenna helped with the search.

   _____

4. on a tuesday, dylan finally found a big clue.

   _____

5. this clue led them up the side of mount jade.

   _____

6. this day in july was hot, and wyatt got tired.

   _____

7. jenna found the treasure behind crystal falls.

   _____

Spellamadoodle

Write each spelling word on the outline of the drawing. You may use the words more than once. For fun, decorate the drawing.

| letter | different | pattern | middle | Mississippi |
| zipper | carry | compass | backpack | river |

The Perfect Treasure

If you found a mystery map, where would you like it to lead? What treasure would you like to find? Describe your perfect treasure below.

✔ **Check Your Writing**

○ I used a capital letter to begin each sentence.

○ I used a capital letter for each proper noun.

○ I checked my spelling.

My Own Mystery Map

Think of a good place at school or in your neighborhood to hide buried treasure. Then write directions for how to find it! Draw a map to go with your directions below.

First, _____ .

Second, _____ .

Third, _____ .

Then, _____ .

Next, _____ .

Last, _____ .

Mystery Map

My Spelling Test

Find the correct answer. Fill in the circle.

1. Which sentence has correct capital letters?
   - ○ fourth of july is my favorite Summer holiday.
   - ○ On saturday, we'll try to find the treasure.
   - ○ Ms. Owens is coming to visit in March.

2. Which noun should be capitalized?
   - ○ brother
   - ○ museum
   - ○ noah

3. Which word is spelled correctly?
   - ○ different
   - ○ diffrent
   - ○ diffrete

4. Which word means "halfway between two things"?
   - ○ pattern
   - ○ middle
   - ○ carry

Ask someone to test you on the spelling words.

1. _____

2. _____

3. _____

4. _____

5. _____

6. _____

7. _____

8. _____

9. _____

10. _____

5. Write the sentence correctly.

   get your cumpass and your bakpak with the zippere

   _____

   _____

Spell & Write • EMC 4539 • © Evan-Moor Corporation

Money Matters

My grandpa is teaching me an important lesson— how to save my money. He has given me fifty dollars for my birthday every year. He takes me to the bank where I have an account. The bank teller puts the money in my account, and she writes the amount in my bankbook. Do you know what the bank does? It pays me for using my money!

Grandpa showed me how to save some money in a change jar, too. I put in quarters, dimes, nickels, and pennies. When the jar is full, I count the money. Then I put it into two piles. I keep one pile to spend, and I take the other to the bank. I like to read my bankbook. I can see my savings grow.

Find It! Read the spelling words.
Check off the words you can find in the story.

✓ again	✓ given	✓ other	✓ does	✓ some
✓ money	✓ change	✓ read	✓ bank	✓ save

How many spelling words did you find? _____

Spelling Practice

Read and Spell	Copy and Spell	Spell It Again!
1. again	_____	_____
2. given	_____	_____
3. other	_____	_____
4. does	_____	_____
5. some	_____	_____
6. money	_____	_____
7. change	_____	_____
8. read	_____	_____
9. bank	_____	_____
10. save	_____	_____

Word Study

Circle the letter or letters in each word that make the sound of o in ton.

> again   does   money
>
> other   some

Unscramble the letters to make spelling words. Write them on the lines.

1. igana _____

2. eghacn _____

3. vgein _____

4. erhot _____

5. nbka _____

6. vesa _____

7. eosd _____

8. yeonm _____

9. edra _____

10. moes _____

Skills:

Spelling Words
with the
Schwa Sound

Spelling
Theme
Vocabulary

Visual Memory

Spelling in
Context

Write It Right

Circle the misspelled words. Write them correctly on the lines.

1. Let's take our munny to the banck.

   _____   _____

2. Mom has givvan me sum coins.

   _____   _____

3. Dous the teller help you make chanje?

   _____   _____

4. I can reade what I sav in my bankbook.

   _____   _____

5. My uther piggy bank is full agane.

   _____   _____

Kinds of Sentences

There are four kinds of sentences. Each kind uses specific ending punctuation.

- A statement tells something. It ends with a period. (.)
- A question asks something. It ends with a question mark. (?)
- A command tells someone to do something. It ends with a period. (.)
- An exclamation shows strong feeling. It ends with an exclamation mark. (!)

Add the correct ending punctuation. Then write whether each sentence is a **statement**, **question**, **command**, or **exclamation**.

1. Did you count all your money _____   _____

2. Put your money in the bank _____   _____

3. Wow, look at all that money _____   _____

4. The bank is behind the library _____   _____

5. Who is the bank teller today _____   _____

6. My house is on fire _____   _____

7. Did you save enough for a coat _____   _____

8. Count this change _____   _____

Make a Match

Draw a line from each spelling word to its meaning.

again   different, not the same

given   performing an action

other   to keep money to use
                         in the future

does   one more time

some   coins, not bills

money   coins and bills people use
                         to buy things

change   an amount that is not named

read   a place where people keep
                         their money

bank   to have handed something
                         to another person

save   to look at written words and
                         understand what they mean

Spellamadoodle

Write each spelling word on the outline of the drawing. You may use the words more than once. For fun, decorate the drawing.

again	given	other	does	some
money	change	read	bank	save

Lots of Money

You just won first place in a contest! You won $10,000! What are you going to do with the money? Buy presents? Save it in the bank? Go on a trip? List ten things you would do with the money.

1. _____

2. _____

3. _____

4. _____

5. _____

6. _____

7. _____

8. _____

9. _____

10. _____

Spell & Write • EMC 4539 • © Evan-Moor Corporation

Lost and Found

You've just found a wallet at the park. It's stuffed full of money!
What will you do with it? Write your story below. Use as many
spelling words as you can.

again	given	other	does	some
money	change	read .	bank	save

✔ Check Your Writing

○ I used a capital letter to begin each sentence.

○ I used correct punctuation at the end of each sentence.

○ I checked my spelling.

My Spelling Test

Find the correct answer. Fill in the circle.

1. What kind of sentence is this?

   Did you save your money in that jar?

   ○ statement
   ○ question
   ○ command
   ○ exclamation

2. What kind of sentence is this?

   Come with me to the bank.

   ○ statement
   ○ question
   ○ command
   ○ exclamation

3. Which word is spelled correctly?

   ○ chanje
   ○ chainge
   ○ change

4. Which word means "different, not the same as mentioned"?

   ○ other
   ○ some
   ○ again

Ask someone to test you on the spelling words.

1. _____

2. _____

3. _____

4. _____

5. _____

6. _____

7. _____

8. _____

9. _____

10. _____

5. Write the sentence correctly.

   they have given me monny to savve in the banck

   _____

   _____

Washington, D.C.

There are many places to see in Washington, D.C. This great city is the capital of the United States. We went with a group of people to see the White House. That is the house where the president lives. The White House was built in 1800! The address is 1600 Pennsylvania Avenue. Around town, there are many parks and museums to visit. We saw a tall white tower named after George Washington. It is called the Washington Monument. We also found a place where you can see airplanes and rockets. It is called the Smithsonian Institute. There are so many things to see in this city. I couldn't see everything. I hope that someday I can visit Washington, D.C., again.

Find It!

Read the spelling words.
Check off the words you can find in the story.

- [ ] town
- [ ] found
- [ ] about
- [ ] house
- [ ] group
- [ ] country
- [ ] around
- [ ] bridge
- [ ] tower
- [ ] park

How many spelling words did you find? _____

Spelling Practice

Read and Spell	Copy and Spell	Spell It Again!
1. town	_____	_____
2. found	_____	_____
3. about	_____	_____
4. house	_____	_____
5. group	_____	_____
6. country	_____	_____
7. around	_____	_____
8. bridge	_____	_____
9. tower	_____	_____
10. park	_____	_____

Rhyme Time

Finish the second line for each poem. Use a spelling word that rhymes with the word in color.

Example: She dropped a pink **flower**,

From the top of the **tower**.

The tiny gray **mouse**,

Lived under our _____.

We heard Barney's lonely **bark**,

All the way across the _____.

I bought an ice-cream **scoop**,

For all the children in our _____.

We looked up, and we looked **down**,

We searched around the entire _____.

We drove along the **ridge**,

Then we came to a high orange _____.

Sound Search

Underline the words with the sound **ow** as in **clown**. Then circle the letters that make the sound.

found   about   park   tower   house

bridge   town   group   country   around

Write the correct words to complete each sentence.

1. Have you _____ the president's _____?

    about   house   group   found

    _____

2. This _____ crosses over to the _____.

    found   around   park   bridge

    _____

3. Our tour _____ climbed up the _____.

    group   house   country   tower

    _____

4. I learned a lot _____ my _____.

    country   about   found   bridge

    _____

5. There is much to see _____ this _____.

    group   town   around   found

    _____

Capital City

Skills:

Using Capital
Letters
Correctly

Writing
Complete
Sentences

> **Use a capital letter to begin:**
>
> - the first word of a sentence
> - the names of days, months, and holidays
> - the word that names yourself—I
> - names of people, pets, and special places
> - people's titles

Circle the letters that should be capitalized.

1. josh wants to visit the grand canyon next year.

_____

2. dr. march lectured about washington, d.c.

_____

3. on saturday, we will visit the lincoln memorial.

_____

4. tanya brought her dog fuzzy to lincoln park.

_____

5. min and i had a barbeque on labor day.

_____

6. mr. kahn gave us a tour of huntington library.

_____

Poetry Time

Create a poem. Write a word or phrase that starts with each letter
in the topic word. Use the words in the story to help you.

V _____

A _____

C _____

A _____

T _____

I _____

O _____

N _____

Spellamadoodle

Write each spelling word on the outline of the drawing. You may use the words more than once. For fun, decorate the drawing.

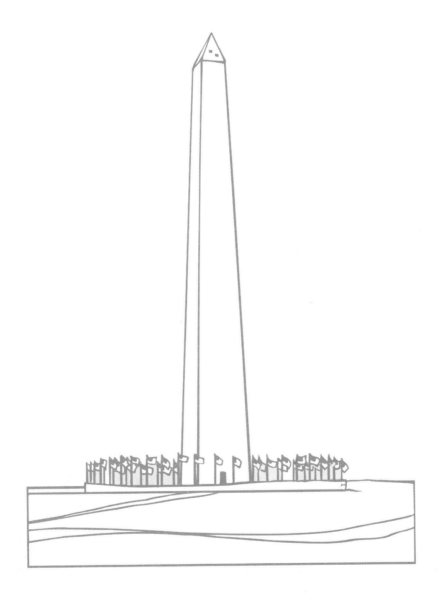

| town | found | about | house | group |
| country | around | bridge | tower | park |

My Favorite Place

Think of a favorite place you've visited. What did you like about it? What do you remember about your trip? Write a journal entry below about one day on your trip. Use as many spelling words as you can.

town	found	about	house	group
country	around	bridge	tower	park

_____

_____

_____

_____

_____

_____

_____

_____

_____

✓ Check Your Writing

○ I used a capital letter at the beginning of each sentence and for each proper noun.

○ I checked my spelling.

Special Vacation

Use the spelling words to complete these paragraphs.

I have _____ so many interesting cities to visit in our _____. One interesting city is San Francisco, California. This city has many landmarks. The Golden Gate Bridge is very famous. The huge orange _____ crosses the bay.

The bridge is near Golden Gate Park. This is a huge _____ where people can visit the Japanese Tea Garden. A _____ of my friends live in a _____ near the park. They like to jog _____ the park.

Another landmark is Coit Tower. This _____ was built to honor the city's firefighters. There are so many interesting things to see and do in San Francisco. I've often thought _____ moving there myself.

town	found	about	house	group
country	around	bridge	tower	park

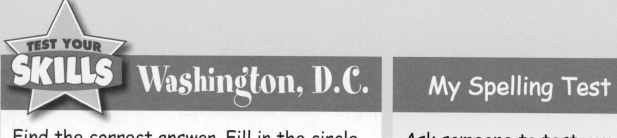

Washington, D.C.

My Spelling Test

Find the correct answer. Fill in the circle.

1. Which sentence has correct capital letters?
   - ○ Mrs. Quinn showed us the Boston Museum of Art.
   - ○ Mrs. quinn showed us the boston Museum of art.
   - ○ mrs. Quinn showed us the Boston museum of art.

2. Which sentence has correct capital letters?
   - ○ jesse and I went to san francisco, california.
   - ○ Jesse and I went to San Francisco, California.
   - ○ Jesse and i went to san francisco, california.

3. Which word is spelled correctly?
   - ○ tower
   - ○ towur
   - ○ touer

4. Which word means "a part of the world with its own borders and government"?
   - ○ bridge
   - ○ town
   - ○ country

Ask someone to test you on the spelling words.

1. _____
2. _____
3. _____
4. _____
5. _____
6. _____
7. _____
8. _____
9. _____
10. _____

5. Write the sentence correctly.

   our growp crossed Lily Bridge on the tour arrownd toun

   _____

   _____

72 **ASSESSMENT 7**

Spell & Write • EMC 4539 • © Evan-Moor Corporation

In the Pond

It's April. It's spring. Time for all the baby animals to come out to play. Quiet! Look over there in the pond. Can you see the ducklings? There are six newborn babies following their mother. The little ducklings are learning how to swim. Mother duck knows how to raise her babies. She shows them where to find delicious duckweed. She also shows them how to dive. Watch those curious ducklings dive among the pond plants. Splash! Splash! A beautiful white swan swims to its nest, and a tiny brown tadpole wiggles to safety. Finally, the baby ducklings waddle home behind their mother. They are going back to their nest. The pond is quiet again.

Find It!

Read the spelling words.
Check off the words you can find in the story.

| ☐ April | ☐ babies | ☐ over | ☐ tiny | ☐ raise |
| ☐ white | ☐ those | ☐ duckweed | ☐ duckling | ☐ tadpole |

How many spelling words did you find? _____

Spelling Practice

Read and Spell

Copy and Spell

Spell It Again!

1. April

2. babies

3. over

4. tiny

5. raise

6. white

7. those

8. duckweed

9. duckling

10. tadpole

Spell & Write • EMC 4539 • © Evan-Moor Corporation

Word Search

Find and circle the spelling words in this word search. Words can go across, down, or diagonally.

```
W  E  A  L  K  D  U  C  E  S  R
I  L  N  D  U  C  K  L  I  N  G
B  A  E  C  K  Y  O  U  B  E  D
A  H  T  S  A  P  R  I  L  O  U
B  W  E  P  D  U  A  K  U  D  C
I  S  H  A  E  B  I  T  O  O  K
E  Y  T  I  N  Y  S  F  V  J  W
S  A  F  E  T  Y  E  E  S  U  E
O  T  H  O  S  E  R  N  I  P  E
W  E  U  L  M  T  P  B  S  E  D
```

Scrambled Words

Unscramble each spelling word and match it to the correct spelling.

isabbe	white
tehiw	April
pAirl	babies
ckgidlnu	duckweed
irsae	tadpole
ytni	duckling
ekwedcud	those
orev	tiny
sehot	over
dotlepa	raise

Awesome Adjectives

Adjectives are words that describe nouns or pronouns.

- An adjective can tell what kind: old **house**
- An adjective can tell which one: that **town**
- An adjective can tell how many: two **ponds**

For each noun, write an adjective that tells what kind.

_____ joke   _____ duckling

_____ pond   _____ sweater

For each noun, write an adjective that tells which one.

_____ swan   _____ fish

_____ park   _____ shoes

For each noun, write an adjective that tells how many.

_____ tadpoles   _____ feathers

_____ babies   _____ books

Skills:

Auditory
Discrimination

Spelling Words
with Long **a**
and Long **i**

Spelling
Theme
Vocabulary

Visual Memory

Word Study

Fill in the missing letters to make spelling words.

tadp ___ ___ e	th ___ s ___	wh ___ t ___

duckw ___ ___ d	r ___ ___ se	d ___ ___ kling

b ___ ___ ies	___ v ___ r	___ ___ ril	t ___ ___ y

Circle the words with the sound a as in bake. Underline the words with the sound i as in smile. Cross out the words with a different sound.

babies	duckling	tadpole
white	those	duckweed
tiny	over	April
		raise

Spellamadoodle

Write each spelling word on the outline of the drawing. You may use the words more than once. For fun, decorate the drawing.

| April | babies | over | tiny | raise |
| white | those | duckweed | duckling | tadpole |

Lost Animal Baby

Pretend you are an animal baby that has gotten separated from its mother. You could be a duckling lost in the tall grasses, or a tadpole fleeing from a hungry swan. What happens to you? Who do you meet? How do you find your mother? Write about it below. Use as many spelling words as you can.

April	babies	over	tiny	raise
white	those	duckweed	duckling	tadpole

Mothers and Babies

Mother animals care for their babies in special ways. Mother ducks teach their babies to swim and find food. Mother frogs produce eggs and swim away. Mother swans teach their cygnets to fly. Choose one animal. Then write about how the mother cares for her babies.

_____

_____

_____

_____

_____

_____

_____

_____

_____

_____

_____

✔ **Check Your Writing**

○ I used complete sentences.

○ I used correct ending punctuation.

○ I checked my spelling.

In the Pond

My Spelling Test

Find the correct answer. Fill in the circle.

1. Which underlined word is an adjective?
   - ○ <u>Tiny</u> tadpoles fill the pond.
   - ○ We took <u>pictures</u> of the ducklings.
   - ○ The ducklings <u>look</u> lost.

2. Which underlined word is an adjective?
   - ○ The <u>tadpoles</u> disappeared.
   - ○ The <u>white</u> swan swam fast.
   - ○ The ducklings <u>learned</u> how to swim.

3. Which word is spelled correctly?
   - ○ rayse
   - ○ raize
   - ○ raise

4. Which word means "very small"?
   - ○ tiny
   - ○ tadpole
   - ○ babies

Ask someone to test you on the spelling words.

1. _____

2. _____

3. _____

4. _____

5. _____

6. _____

7. _____

8. _____

9. _____

10. _____

5. Write the sentence correctly.

can thoz wite duck babys find the pond

_____

_____

Spell & Write • EMC 4539 • © Evan-Moor Corporation

Zoo Quiz

Is your favorite animal at the zoo

Smarter than an elephant?

Smarter than you?

More useful than a monkey

Or a chimpanzee or two?

More fearless than a lion?

More careless than a kangaroo?

Which one is the happiest?

The snake? The bear? The gnu?

Which one is the funniest?

Or fastest at the zoo?

I think I like the tiger.

Do you have a favorite, too?

Tell me, yes, please do!

Find It!

Read the spelling words.
Check off the words you can find in the story.

☐ useful	☐ smarter	☐ fastest	☐ funniest	☐ happiest
☐ fearless	☐ careless	☐ feed	☐ clean	☐ animal

How many spelling words did you find? _____

Spelling Practice

Read and Spell

Copy and Spell

Spell It Again!

1. useful

2. smarter

3. fastest

4. funniest

5. happiest

6. fearless

7. careless

8. feed

9. clean

10. animal

Find the Words

Write the missing words to complete the sentences.

1. Do you think cheetahs are _____ or _____?

  animal　　　　fastest　　　　happiest　　　　feed

_____

2. Zookeepers _____ and _____ the animals.

  fearless　　　　useful　　　　feed　　　　clean

_____

3. The lion is said to be a _____ _____.

  animal　　　　funniest　　　　fearless　　　　fastest

_____

4. I think elephants are _____ than zebras.

  useful　　　　clean　　　　smarter　　　　careless

_____

5. Many animals are _____ to humans.

  happiest　　　　smarter　　　　feed　　　　useful

_____

6. Monkeys are the _____ animals in the zoo!

  feed　　　　clean　　　　funniest　　　　animal

_____

Skills:

Spelling Words
with Suffixes
**–ful, –er, –est,
–less**

Spelling
Theme
Vocabulary

Matching
Words
with Their
Meanings

What Does It Mean?

Look at the meanings of the suffixes in the box. Then write the spelling word for each definition.

less = without	ful = full of	er = more	est = most

| useful | smarter | fastest | funniest | happiest |
| fearless | careless | feed | clean | animal |

1. more intelligent _____

2. most happy _____

3. without care _____

4. most fast _____

5. full of use _____

6. without fear _____

7. most funny _____

Comparing Words

> An adjective tells about a noun. An adjective can make comparisons.
>
> - Use er to compare two people, places, or things.
>
>   **Elephants are taller than zebras.**
>
> - Use est to compare three or more people, places, or things.
>
>   **Giraffes are the tallest animals in the zoo.**

Write the correct adjective in the blank.

1. The zookeeper is the _____ person in the zoo.

   smarter   smartest

2. The green snakes are _____ than the striped snakes.

   longer   longest

3. The toucan has _____ feathers than the flamingo.

   brighter   brightest

4. Simba the lion is the _____ in his pride.

   larger   largest

5. That is the _____ roar I've ever heard!

   louder   loudest

6. Champ the chimp is the _____ monkey here.

   older   oldest

Make a Match

Write the letter of the definition next to the word.

_____ 1. useful   a. not paying close attention

_____ 2. fearless   b. to give food to

_____ 3. smarter   c. causing the most laughter

_____ 4. careless   d. free from dirt

_____ 5. fastest   e. helpful

_____ 6. feed   f. a living thing that is not a plant

_____ 7. funniest   g. most cheerful

_____ 8. clean   h. unafraid

_____ 9. happiest   i. more intelligent or clever

_____ 10. animal   j. moving the quickest

Spellamadoodle

Write each spelling word on the outline of the drawing. You may use the words more than once. For fun, decorate the drawing.

useful	smarter	fastest	funniest	happiest
fearless	careless	feed	clean	animal

Zoo Questions

Use words from "Zoo Quiz" to answer these questions about zoo animals.

1. Which zoo animal do you think is smart?

_____

_____

2. Which zoo animal do you think is fearless?

_____

_____

3. Which zoo animal do you think is fast?

_____

_____

4. Which zoo animal do you think is funny?

_____

_____

5. Which zoo animal do you think is useful?

_____

_____

Backyard Zoo

The zookeeper said you could bring home three animals from the zoo! Which animals would you choose? Describe how you would keep and care for them. Use some of the spelling words.

useful	smarter	fastest	funniest	happiest
fearless	careless	feed	clean	animal

✓ **Check Your Writing**

○ I used complete sentences.

○ I used commas correctly.

○ I checked my spelling.

Zoo Quiz

My Spelling Test

Find the correct answer. Fill in the circle.

1. Which adjective correctly completes this sentence?

   Jenny's cat is _____ than her dog.
   - ○ fluffy
   - ○ fluffier
   - ○ fluffiest

2. Which adjective correctly completes this sentence?

   Which giraffe's neck is the _____ in the group?
   - ○ long
   - ○ longer
   - ○ longest

3. Which word is spelled correctly?
   - ○ happyest
   - ○ happiess
   - ○ happiest

4. Which word means "free from dirt"?
   - ○ clean
   - ○ feed
   - ○ useful

Ask someone to test you on the spelling words.

1. _____
2. _____
3. _____
4. _____
5. _____
6. _____
7. _____
8. _____
9. _____
10. _____

5. Write the sentence correctly.

   i think the feerliss lion is a smarttr annimul than the zebra

   _____

   _____

Spell & Write • EMC 4539 • © Evan-Moor Corporation

Breakfast Is Served

On Saturday morning, my older brother Chris and I got up early. We wanted to make a surprise breakfast for our mother. I helped measure the milk, and then Chris showed me how to break the eggs. We cut up some bread cubes and put them in a baking dish. We poured the milk and eggs over the bread, and I sprinkled on some cheese. Then it was time for baking. I put it in the oven for twenty minutes. When Mom heard the timer go off, she came into the kitchen. Was she surprised to find a delicious breakfast ready to eat!

Find It! Read the spelling words.
Check off the words you can find in the story.

| ☐ early | ☐ heard | ☐ friend | ☐ eat | ☐ measure |
| ☐ break | ☐ brother | ☐ mother | ☐ bread | ☐ oven |

How many spelling words did you find? _____

Spelling Practice

Read and Spell | Copy and Spell | Spell It Again!

1. early

2. heard

3. friend

4. eat

5. measure

6. break

7. brother

8. mother

9. bread

10. oven

Spell It

Circle the word in each row that is spelled correctly.

1.   hurd   heard   herde

2.   ovven   ovun   oven

3.   muther   mother   mothre

4.   friend   frend   freind

5.   eat   eet   eate

6.   erly   urley   early

7.   mesurre   measure   meassur

8.   brother   bruther   broethr

9.   brak   breek   break

10. bread   brede   breadd

Skills:

Spelling Words
with **ea**

Spelling
Theme
Vocabulary

Matching
Words
with Their
Meanings

Crossword Challenge

Complete the crossword puzzle using the spelling words.

| early | heard | friend | eat | measure |
| break | brother | mother | bread | oven |

Down

1. a boy or man who has the same parents as another person
2. to have sensed sounds through your ears
4. a baked food made from flour, water, and often yeast
5. an enclosed space where food is baked or roasted
6. a female parent
7. before the usual time

Across

3. someone whom you know well and enjoy being with
6. to find out the size, capacity, or weight of something
8. to take in food through the mouth
9. to damage something so that it is in pieces

Action and Helping Verbs

A **verb** tells what is happening to the noun.
- **Action verbs** show an action.

measure, cook, break, eat

- **Helping verbs** come before the main verb to tell about the action.

will, has, had, have, could, would, should, do, does, did

Write the correct verb in the blank. Then write **A** for **action** or **H** for **helping** in the box after the sentence.

1. In the morning, I _____ the warm sun on my face.

    sleep   would   feel

_____

2. Let's _____ breakfast for Mother.

    make   should   am

_____

3. I know he _____ snooze and snore.

    was   have   will

_____

4. Eggs and bacon _____ in the pan.

    sizzle   am   will

_____

5. We _____ make tasty pancakes, too.

    does   could   is

_____

Word Study

Say each word aloud. Then write it next to the correct sound.

| heard | measure | eat | bread | break | early |

1. **a** as in **bake** _____

2. **e** as in **bed** _____   _____

3. **ir** as in **bird** _____   _____

4. **e** as in **weak** _____

Fill in the missing letters.

1. br ____ th ____ ____

2. fr ____ ____ nd

3. m ____ th ____ ____

4. ____ v ____ n

Spellamadoodle

Write each spelling word on the outline of the drawing. You may use the words more than once. For fun, decorate the drawing.

| early | heard | friend | eat | measure |
| break | brother | mother | bread | oven |

My Favorite Recipe

What is a favorite food that you can make yourself? Write your favorite recipe below. Remember to write the steps in order.

Recipe for: _____

You will need:

_____   _____

_____   _____

_____

1. _____

_____

2. _____

_____

3. _____

_____

4. _____

_____

5. _____

_____

6. _____

_____

Special Gift

The children in the story are making a special breakfast for their mother. What special gifts have you received? Write about a time when someone gave you a wonderful gift.

_____

_____

_____

_____

_____

_____

_____

_____

_____

_____

_____

_____

✔ **Check Your Writing**

○ I wrote complete sentences.

○ I used correct punctuation.

○ I checked my spelling.

My Spelling Test

Find the correct answer. Fill in the circle.

1. In which sentence is the underlined word an action verb?
   - ○ Shania <u>is</u> an excellent cook.
   - ○ Shania <u>has</u> big dreams.
   - ○ Shania <u>bakes</u> delicious pies.

2. In which sentence is the helping verb underlined?
   - ○ Trey <u>will</u> make dinner tonight.
   - ○ He <u>likes</u> steak and baked potatoes.
   - ○ We <u>brought</u> the dessert.

3. Which word is spelled correctly?
   - ○ meazhur
   - ○ measure
   - ○ meshure

4. Which word means "an enclosed space where food is baked"?
   - ○ oven
   - ○ eat
   - ○ bread

Ask someone to test you on the spelling words.

1. _____

2. _____

3. _____

4. _____

5. _____

6. _____

7. _____

8. _____

9. _____

10. _____

5. Write the sentence correctly.

   muthr's frends is coming eurly to bake bredd

   _____

   _____

Once upon a Time

Long, long ago, Princess Dahlia sat in her room in the castle. On this dreamy night, Dahlia thought about her future. She wished to be a squire, just like her brother. Then someday, she could become a knight! Dahlia loved each story about the knights' bravery as they brought peace to the land. Their skills in war were unmatched. Their adventures seemed endless. Dahlia longed to have her own adventures out there in the world. She closed her eyes to think what her life might be like. Suddenly, she felt something enter her room. When Dahlia opened her eyes, the room was full of golden light.

She was dressed in a suit of shining armor! A shield was ready at her side. She was about to begin a new adventure!

Find It! Read the spelling words.
Check off the words you can find in the story.

war	night	knight	piece	peace
their	there	castle	story	princess

How many spelling words did you find? _____

Skills:

Homophones

Spelling
Theme
Vocabulary

Visual Memory

Spelling Practice

Read and Spell

Copy and Spell

Spell It Again!

1. war

2. night

3. knight

4. piece

5. peace

6. their

7. there

8. castle

9. story

10. princess

Sound Search

Say the words in the box aloud. Write the two words that sound the same on the lines.

night	peace	there	wore
piece	their	war	knight

1. _____

_____

2. _____

_____

3. _____

_____

4. _____

_____

What spelling word means the opposite of _____?

war _____

here _____

day _____

What spelling word means the same as _____?

part _____

tale _____

belonging to them _____

Skills:

Homophones

Spelling
Theme
Vocabulary

Visual Memory

Super Spellings

Circle the word that correctly completes each sentence.

1. It was a dark, starry knight/night.

2. The knight/night wore a suit of shining armor.

3. They spread peace/piece across the land.

4. A peace/piece of her dream came true.

5. She saw the shield their/there in the corner.

6. The knights gave their/there all to the war.

Circle the words that are spelled correctly.

peece	story	prinsces	cassle
castle	nitek	night	peace
wor	ther	war	princess
their	peice	there	night

Correcting Capitals

Correct the words that need capital letters. Cross out the small letter and write the capital letter above it.

july	morning	dr. barns
labor day	thursday	week
mr. gonzales	sister	brett
teacher	ms. spencer	halloween

Circle the letters that should be capitalized. Then rewrite the sentences.

1. at night, the princess dreamed of king william.

   _____

2. is saturday dahlia's favorite day of the week?

   _____

3. "i practice sword fighting on tuesdays," the knight said.

   _____

4. the gallant prince john rode the white steed.

   _____

5. "would you like to be a squire?" the fairy asked.

   _____

Word Search

Find and circle the spelling words. Words can go across, down, or diagonally.

war	night	knight	piece	peace
their	there	castle	story	princess

```
T E N D E R H A R T O T
T O P I E C E Z H A N D
H H E R U G S G O T D N
E O G H I P I N O L D A
I B S I S N O R A Y O L
R O S E N O C W A R E G
P E A C E K O E X O L N
I A T A N K C A S T L E
E R E H T H E N O S E S
```

Spell & Write • EMC 4539 • © Evan-Moor Corporation

Spellamadoodle

Write each spelling word on the outline of the drawing. You may use the words more than once. For fun, decorate the drawing.

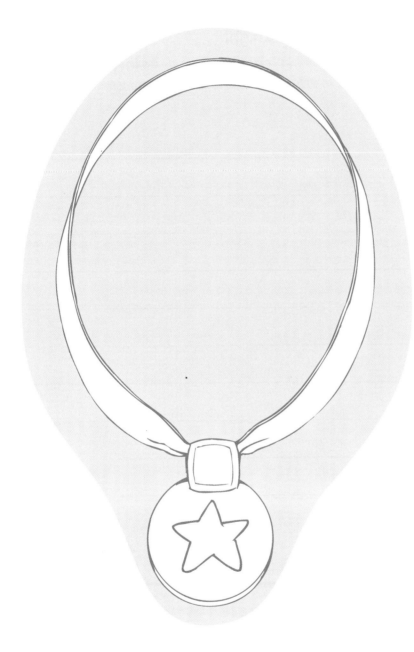

war	night	knight	piece	peace
their	there	castle	story	princess

What Happened Next?

What do you think happened to Dahlia after she got her suit of armor and her shield? Write about her new adventures. Use as many spelling words as you can.

war	night	knight	piece	peace
their	there	castle	story	princess

_____

_____

_____

_____

_____

_____

_____

_____

_____

_____

✔ **Check Your Writing**

○ I used capital letters correctly.

○ I wrote complete sentences.

○ I checked my spelling.

The Perfect Knight

Knights in the Middle Ages lived by a strict code. This code included rules about honor and bravery. What do you think are important skills for a knight to have? Strong? Polite? Brave? List eight skills below.

1. _____

2. _____

3. _____

4. _____

5. _____

6. _____

7. _____

8. _____

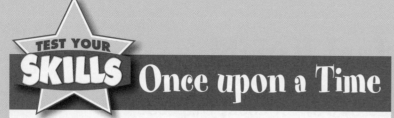

Once upon a Time

My Spelling Test

Find the correct answer. Fill in the circle.

1. Which sentence has correct capital letters?
   - ○ king george knighted james on Sunday.
   - ○ King george Knighted James on sunday.
   - ○ King George knighted James on Sunday.

2. Which sentence has correct capital letters?
   - ○ dahlia wanted to be a knight for halloween.
   - ○ Dahlia wanted to be a knight for halloween.
   - ○ Dahlia wanted to be a knight for Halloween.

3. Which word is spelled correctly?
   - ○ castle
   - ○ cassle
   - ○ cassel

4. Which word means "the time between sunset and sunrise"?
   - ○ story
   - ○ war
   - ○ night

Ask someone to test you on the spelling words.

1. _____

2. _____

3. _____

4. _____

5. _____

6. _____

7. _____

8. _____

9. _____

10. _____

5. Write the sentence correctly.

the knite's storey of peese spread through the land

_____

_____

Spell & Write • EMC 4539 • © Evan-Moor Corporation

Postcard from Mexico

Dear Jordan,

Here is your postcard from Mexico. We are having a really fun vacation. The beach here is beautiful, and the sand is white like sugar. The air is so warm that we can wear our summer clothes, even at night! The people are friendly, too.

Yesterday we rented a sailboat. You should have seen the color of the ocean. It was bright blue, and we could see all the way to the bottom! The water was as warm as a bath. Every day, we eat all of our favorite Mexican foods. This is a vacation to remember. Wish you were here!

**Your friend,
Ana**

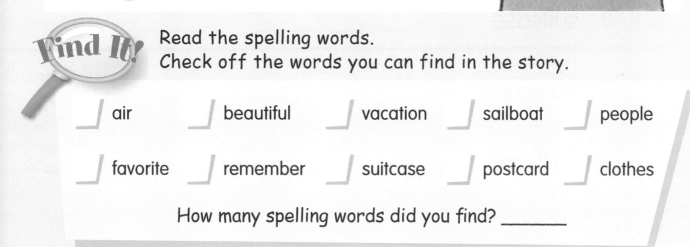

Find It! Read the spelling words.
Check off the words you can find in the story.

☐ air	☐ beautiful	☐ vacation	☐ sailboat	☐ people
☐ favorite	☐ remember	☐ suitcase	☐ postcard	☐ clothes

How many spelling words did you find? _____

Spelling Practice

Read and Spell	Copy and Spell	Spell It Again!
1. air	_____	_____
2. beautiful	_____	_____
3. favorite	_____	_____
4. clothes	_____	_____
5. people	_____	_____
6. vacation	_____	_____
7. remember	_____	_____
8. suitcase	_____	_____
9. postcard	_____	_____
10. sailboat	_____	_____

Circle and Spell

Circle the word in each row that is spelled correctly.

1.	clothes	clothz	cloese
2.	sutecas	suitcase	sootcase
3.	butiful	beautiful	beutifull
4.	peeple	pepole	people
5.	air	aer	aire
6.	postkerd	posttcarde	postcard
7.	faverit	favorite	faverote
8.	remember	remmembr	rememmber
9.	salebote	saillboate	sailboat
10.	vacation	vakashion	vacasion

Building Words

Skills:

Compound
Words

Spelling
Theme
Vocabulary

Visual Memory

Fill in the missing letters to make spelling words.

1.	b ___ ___ utif ___ l	6.	s ___ ___ tc ___ se
2.	cl ___ ___ ___ es	7.	p ___ ___ pl ___
3.	___ ___ r	8.	rem ___ ___ b ___ r
4.	fav ___ ___ ___ te	9.	postc ___ ___ ___
5.	s ___ ___ lbo ___ t	10.	vaca ___ ___ ___ n

Draw a line between the words to make compound spelling words. Write the words on the lines.

sail   card   _____

suit   boat   _____

post   case   _____

Word Search

Find and circle the spelling words. Words can go across, down,
or diagonally.

air	beautiful	favorite	clothes	people
vacation	remember	suitcase	postcard	sailboat

```
W  T  E  P  O  S  T  C  A  R  D  C
S  A  I  L  B  O  A  T  L  S  P  S
R  C  P  S  T  Q  E  U  H  Y  E  V
E  A  E  L  U  A  F  R  Y  H  I  A
F  A  V  O  R  I  T  E  T  D  E  C
R  U  I  A  T  R  T  O  I  L  R  A
I  E  W  U  H  Y  L  C  P  J  S  T
S  L  A  C  N  C  R  O  A  E  P  I
R  E  M  E  M  B  E  R  T  S  O  O
B  R  O  A  T  P  R  U  B  S  E  N
```

When Did It Happen?

A **verb** can show action. The tense of a verb tells when an action occurs.

- present—the action is happening now.

    We **are** swimming.

- past—the action already happened.

    I **swam** yesterday.

- future—the action is going to happen.

    Tomorrow I **will** swim.

Rewrite this sentence in the present tense and then the past tense.

Tanya will write a postcard to her friend.

1. _____

2. _____

Rewrite this sentence in the past tense and then the future tense.

Marco feels the warm sand between his toes.

1. _____

2. _____

Rewrite this sentence in the present and then the future tense.

Jake and Kaitlin sailed on their vacation.

1. _____

2. _____

Spellamadoodle

Write each spelling word on the outline of the drawing. You may use the words more than once. For fun, decorate the drawing.

| air | beautiful | favorite | clothes | people |
| vacation | remember | suitcase | postcard | sailboat |

Postcard to a Friend

What kinds of trips have you taken? Have you visited a museum, the zoo, or the beach? Write a postcard to a friend telling about your trip. Use as many spelling words as you can.

air	beautiful	favorite	clothes	people
vacation	remember	suitcase	postcard	sailboat

To:_____

_____

_____

✔ **Check Your Writing**

○ I used a capital letter to begin each sentence.

○ I wrote complete sentences.

○ I checked my spelling.

My Favorite Places

On the postcard, Ana describes Mexico to her friend. Think of three of your favorite places. Describe what you like about each place.

Favorite Place #1: _____

_____

_____

_____

_____

Favorite Place #2: _____

_____

_____

_____

_____

Favorite Place #3: _____

_____

_____

_____

_____

Postcard from Mexico

My Spelling Test

Find the correct answer. Fill in the circle.

1. Which tense is the verb in this sentence?

   Jordan will read his postcard after school.

   ○ past
   ○ present
   ○ future

2. Which tense is the verb in this sentence?

   Ana travels to Mexico every summer.

   ○ past
   ○ present
   ○ future

3. Which word is spelled correctly?

   ○ sailboat
   ○ sailbote
   ○ saillboate

4. Which word means "the mixture of gases that surround the Earth"?

   ○ people
   ○ air
   ○ beautiful

Ask someone to test you on the spelling words.

1. _____

2. _____

3. _____

4. _____

5. _____

6. _____

7. _____

8. _____

9. _____

10. _____

5. Write the sentence correctly.

   remumbr to bring your fovurit clothz

   _____

   _____

Spell & Write • EMC 4539 • © Evan-Moor Corporation

Test Your Skills–Record Form

Unit	Test Page	Topic	Test Your Skills Score (5 possible)	Spelling Test Score (10 possible)
1	12	Let's Go Camping!		
2	22	At the Library		
3	32	Sports, Sports, Sports		
4	42	Family Rap		
5	52	Mystery Map		
6	62	Money Matters		
7	72	Washington, D.C.		
8	82	In the Pond		
9	92	Zoo Quiz		
10	102	Breakfast Is Served		
11	112	Once upon a Time		
12	122	Postcard from Mexico		

Pull-out Spelling Lists

Use these lists to give spelling tests, post on the refrigerator, and for extra practice.

Unit 1 Let's Go Camping!	Unit 2 At the Library	Unit 3 Sports, Sports, Sports
1. pitch	1. next	1. point
2. drink	2. left	2. coach
3. swim	3. help	3. tie
4. which	4. please	4. everybody
5. light	5. believe	5. everyone
6. while	6. many	6. outside
7. find	7. between	7. basketball
8. fire	8. order	8. skateboard
9. tent	9. author	9. earthquake
10. camp	10. title	10. homework

Pull-out Spelling Lists

Use these lists to give spelling tests, post on the refrigerator, and for extra practice.

Unit 4 Family Rap	Unit 5 Mystery Map	Unit 6 Money Matters
1. I'm	1. letter	1. again
2. it's	2. different	2. given
3. they're	3. pattern	3. other
4. we're	4. middle	4. does
5. that's	5. Mississippi	5. some
6. o'clock	6. zipper	6. money
7. let's	7. carry	7. change
8. together	8. compass	8. read
9. home	9. backpack	9. bank
10. family	10. river	10. save

Pull-out Spelling Lists

Use these lists to give spelling tests, post on the refrigerator, and for extra practice.

Unit 7 Washington, D.C.	Unit 8 In the Pond	Unit 9 Zoo Quiz
1. town	1. April	1. useful
2. found	2. babies	2. smarter
3. about	3. over	3. fastest
4. house	4. tiny	4. funniest
5. group	5. raise	5. happiest
6. country	6. white	6. fearless
7. around	7. those	7. careless
8. bridge	8. duckweed	8. feed
9. tower	9. duckling	9. clean
10. park	10. tadpole	10. animal

Pull-out Spelling Lists

Use these lists to give spelling tests, post on the refrigerator, and for extra practice.

Unit 10 Breakfast Is Served	Unit 11 Once upon a Time	Unit 12 Postcard from Mexico
1. early	1. war	1. air
2. heard	2. night	2. beautiful
3. friend	3. knight	3. favorite
4. eat	4. piece	4. clothes
5. measure	5. peace	5. people
6. break	6. their	6. vacation
7. brother	7. there	7. remember
8. mother	8. castle	8. suitcase
9. bread	9. story	9. postcard
10. oven	10. princess	10. sailboat

Spell & Write • EMC 4539 • © Evan-Moor Corporation

Answer Key

Page 3

Let's Go Camping!

My family likes to camp in the mountains every summer. We find a good spot near the lake to pitch our tent. That makes it easy to swim whenever we like. My brother and I look for firewood while Mom and Dad set up camp. Then we light a big fire. My family tells stories around the fire until we can't stay awake any longer. The next day, we pack a lunch. We get water to drink. We have a new boat this year. It's bigger than our old boat. We can't wait to put our boat in the lake. We'll sail over to Pine Island to go exploring. I wonder what we'll find?

Find It! Read the spelling words. Check off the words you can find in the story.

| ✓ pitch | ✓ drink | ✓ swim | ✓ while | ✓ light |
| ✓ which | ✓ find | ✓ fire | ✓ tent | ✓ camp |

How many spelling words did you find? __9__

Page 5

Find the Words

Write the missing spelling words to complete the sentences.

1. Let's __pitch__ our __tent__ near the lake.
   which / tent / pitch

2. I can __swim__ __while__ you fish for dinner.
   while / swim / tent

3. We will __light__ the __fire__ to toast marshmallows.
   pitch / fire / light

4. Did you __find__ a good place to __camp__?
   drink / find / camp

5. That __drink__ __which__ is sweet, tastes good!
   which / tent / drink

Page 6

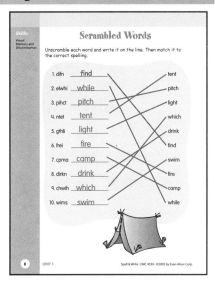

Scrambled Words

Unscramble each word and write it on the line. Then match it to the correct spelling.

1. difn __find__
2. elwhi __while__
3. pihct __pitch__
4. ntet __tent__
5. gthli __light__
6. frei __fire__
7. cpma __camp__
8. dirkn __drink__
9. chwih __which__
10. wims __swim__

tent / pitch / light / which / drink / find / swim / fire / camp / while

Page 7

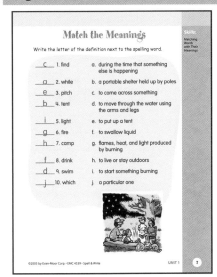

Match the Meanings

Write the letter of the definition next to the spelling word.

__c__ 1. find — a. during the time that something else is happening
__a__ 2. while — b. a portable shelter held up by poles
__e__ 3. pitch — c. to come across something
__b__ 4. tent — d. to move through the water using the arms and legs
__i__ 5. light — e. to put up a tent
__g__ 6. fire — f. to swallow liquid
__h__ 7. camp — g. flames, heat, and light produced by burning
__f__ 8. drink — h. to live or stay outdoors
__d__ 9. swim — i. to start something burning
__j__ 10. which — j. a particular one

Page 8

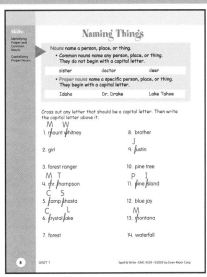

Naming Things

Nouns name a person, place, or thing.
• Common nouns name any person, place, or thing. They do not begin with a capital letter.

sister   doctor   deer

• Proper nouns name a specific person, place, or thing. They begin with a capital letter.

Idaho   Dr. Drake   Lake Tahoe

Cross out any letter that should be a capital letter. Then write the capital letter above it.

1. mount whitney — M W
2. girl
3. forest ranger
4. mr. thompson — M T
5. camp shasta — C S
6. crystal lake — C L
7. forest
8. brother
9. justin — J
10. pine tree
11. pine island — P I
12. blue jay
13. montana — M
14. waterfall

Page 10

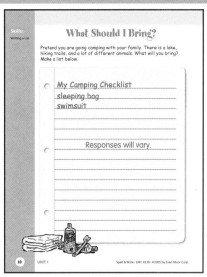

What Should I Bring?

Pretend you are going camping with your family. There is a lake, hiking trails, and a lot of different animals. What will you bring? Make a list below.

My Camping Checklist
sleeping bag
swimsuit

Responses will vary.

Page 11

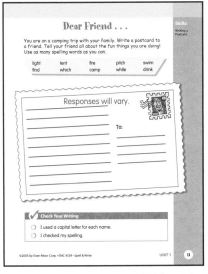

Dear Friend . . .

You are on a camping trip with your family. Write a postcard to a friend. Tell your friend all about the fun things you are doing! Use as many spelling words as you can.

| light | tent | fire | pitch | swim |
| find | which | camp | while | drink |

Responses will vary.
To:

Check Your Writing
○ I used a capital letter for each name.
○ I checked my spelling.

Page 12

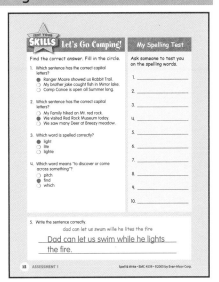

TEST YOUR SKILLS — **Let's Go Camping!**   **My Spelling Test**

Find the correct answer. Fill in the circle.

Ask someone to test you on the spelling words.

1. Which sentence has the correct capital letters?
   ● Ranger Moore showed us Rabbit Trail.
   ○ My brother jake caught fish in Mirror lake.
   ○ Camp Canoe is open all Summer long.

2. Which sentence has the correct capital letters?
   ○ My Family hiked on Mt. red rock.
   ● We visited Red Rock Museum today.
   ○ We saw many Deer at Breezy meadow.

3. Which word is spelled correctly?
   ● light
   ○ lite
   ○ lighte

4. Which word means "to discover or come across something"?
   ○ pitch
   ● find
   ○ which

5. Write the sentence correctly.
   dad can let us swum wille he lites the fire
   __Dad can let us swim while he lights the fire.__

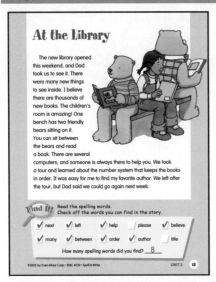

At the Library

The new library opened this weekend, and Dad took us to see it. There were many new things to see inside. I believe there are thousands of new books. The children's room is amazing! One bench has two friendly bears sitting on it. You can sit between the bears and read a book. There are several computers, and someone is always there to help you. We took a tour and learned about the number system that keeps the books in order. It was easy for me to find my favorite author. We left after the tour, but Dad said we could go again next week.

Find It Read the spelling words. Check off the words you can find in the story.

✓ next ✓ left ✓ help ☐ please ✓ believe
✓ many ✓ between ✓ order ✓ author ☐ title

How many spelling words did you find? __8__

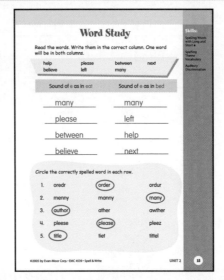

Word Study

Read the words. Write them in the correct column. One word will be in both columns.

help   please   between   next
believe   left   many

Sound of e as in eat	Sound of e as in bed
many	many
please	left
between	help
believe	next

Circle the correctly spelled word in each row.

1. oredr (order) ordur
2. menny manny (many)
3. (author) ather awther
4. pleese (please) pleez
5. (title) tiet tittel

Spelling Words

Fill in the missing letters to make spelling words.

next   left   help   please   believe
many   between   order   author   title

1. pl_e_ _a_ se
2. l_e_ ft
3. betw_e_ _e_ n
4. m_a_ ny
5. n_e_ xt
6. t_i_ t_l_ e
7. _o_ r der
8. h_e_ lp
9. bel_i_ _e_ ve
10. _a_ _u_ thor

Picking Pronouns

A *pronoun* is a word that takes the place of one or more nouns.

Jenna works at the library.   She works at the library.

Use the pronouns below to replace the underlined words. Write the pronouns on the line. You will use some pronouns more than once.

he   she   you   it   they   them

1. I believe <u>Tanya</u> checked out that book already. __she__
2. You can find <u>books</u> on many shelves. __them__
3. Chad likes books about <u>dinosaurs</u>. __them__
4. <u>My mom</u> read aloud books to the children. __She__
5. <u>Children</u> can sit between the bears to read. __They__
6. Please help me look up titles on the <u>computer</u>. __it__
7. <u>These books</u> are in a certain order. __They__
8. <u>Dad</u> left us in the children's room to read. __He__

Which Word?

Write the missing words on the lines.

1. Margie chose her book __next__
   believe   next   help
2. Trey is the __author__ of this book.
   many   please   author
3. Can you read the __title__ of this book?
   title   between   many
4. Dad will __help__ us at the library.
   help   author   title
5. Jack sat __between__ both bears on the bench.
   please   next   between
6. I found so __many__ books at the new library.
   many   please   author
7. We __left__ after the tour.
   order   left   please
8. I learned what __order__ the books are in.
   please   left   order

My Favorite Books

Do you visit the library often? What are some of the books you've read? List the titles of your three favorite books. Then write what each book was about.

My **3** Favorites

1. Title __Responses will vary.__
2. Title
3. Title

Library Visit

Have you been to the library? What do you like to do there? How do you find the books you want? Describe a trip to the library. Use as many spelling words as you can.

next   left   help   please   believe
many   between   order   author   title

Responses will vary.

✓ **Check Your Writing**
○ I used a capital letter to begin each sentence.
○ I used a period to end each sentence.
○ I checked my spelling.

At the Library

Find the correct answer. Fill in the circle.

1. Which pronoun would you use to replace the word **Maria**?
   ○ the
   ● she
   ○ they

2. Which pronoun would you use to replace **the computer**?
   ○ she
   ○ they
   ● it

3. Which word is spelled correctly?
   ● many
   ○ meny
   ○ manny

4. Which word means "the writer of a book, play, or poem"?
   ○ title
   ● author
   ○ order

5. Write the sentence correctly.
   we believes this titel is nekst for our author
   __We believe this title is next for__
   __our author.__

My Spelling Test

Ask someone to test you on the spelling words.

1. _____
2. _____
3. _____
4. _____
5. _____
6. _____
7. _____
8. _____
9. _____
10. _____

Page 23

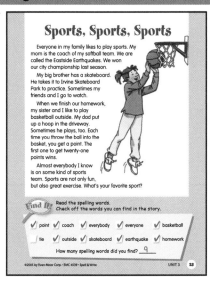

Sports, Sports, Sports

Everyone in my family likes to play sports. My mom is the coach of my softball team. We are called the Eastside Earthquakes. We won our city championship last season.

My big brother has a skateboard. He takes it to Irvine Skateboard Park to practice. Sometimes my friends and I go to watch.

When we finish our homework, my sister and I like to play basketball outside. My dad put up a hoop in the driveway. Sometimes he plays, too. Each time you throw the ball into the basket, you get a point. The first one to get twenty-one points wins.

Almost everybody I know is on some kind of sports team. Sports are not only fun, but also great exercise. What's your favorite sport?

Find it! Read the spelling words. Check off the words you can find in the story.

☑ point ☑ coach ☑ everybody ☑ everyone ☑ basketball
☐ tie ☑ outside ☑ skateboard ☑ earthquake ☑ homework

How many spelling words did you find? _9_

©2005 by Evan-Moor Corp. • EMC 4539 • Spell & Write   UNIT 3   23

Page 25

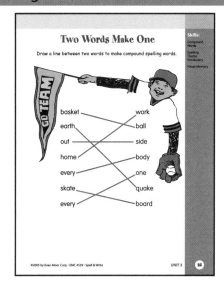

Two Words Make One

Draw a line between two words to make compound spelling words.

basket — work
earth — ball
out — side
home — body
every — one
skate — quake
every — board

©2005 by Evan-Moor Corp. • EMC 4539 • Spell & Write   UNIT 3   25

Page 26

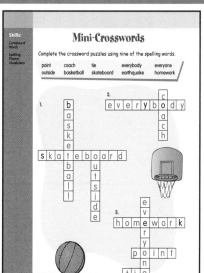

Mini-Crosswords

Complete the crossword puzzles using nine of the spelling words.

point coach tie everybody everyone
outside basketball skateboard earthquake homework

Page 27

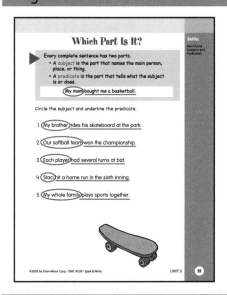

Which Part Is It?

Every complete sentence has two parts.
- A subject is the part that names the main person, place, or thing.
- A predicate is the part that tells what the subject is or does.

(My mom) bought me a basketball.

Circle the subject and underline the predicate.

1. (My brother) rides his skateboard at the park.
2. (Our softball team) won the championship.
3. (Each player) had several turns at bat.
4. (Staci) hit a home run in the sixth inning.
5. (My whole family) plays sports together.

©2005 by Evan-Moor Corp. • EMC 4539 • Spell & Write   UNIT 3   27

Page 28

Make a Match

Write the letter of the definition next to the word.

e 1. point
i 2. outside
a 3. coach
g 4. basketball
h 5. tie
c 6. skateboard
d 7. everyone/everybody
b 8. earthquake
f 9. homework

a. one who trains a sports team
b. sudden violent shaking of the earth
c. board with wheels that you stand on and ride
d. each and every person
e. unit for scoring in a game
f. schoolwork done at home
g. game played by 2 teams of 5 players each
h. when 2 teams have the same score
i. out of a building, or in the open air

28   UNIT 3   Spell & Write • EMC 4539 • ©2005 by Evan-Moor Corp.

Page 30

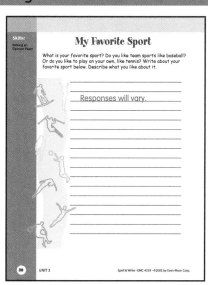

My Favorite Sport

What is your favorite sport? Do you like team sports like baseball? Or do you like to play on your own, like tennis? Write about your favorite sport below. Describe what you like about it.

Responses will vary.

30   UNIT 3   Spell & Write • EMC 4539 • ©2005 by Evan-Moor Corp.

Page 31

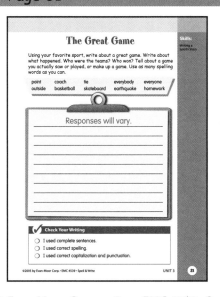

The Great Game

Using your favorite sport, write about a great game. Write about what happened. Who were the teams? Who won? Tell about a game you actually saw or played, or make up a game. Use as many spelling words as you can.

point coach tie everybody everyone
outside basketball skateboard earthquake homework

Responses will vary.

✓ Check Your Writing
○ I used complete sentences.
○ I used correct spelling.
○ I used correct capitalization and punctuation.

©2005 by Evan-Moor Corp. • EMC 4539 • Spell & Write   UNIT 3   31

Page 32

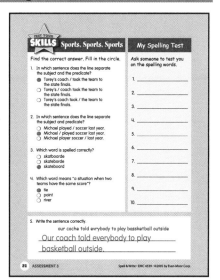

TEST YOUR SKILLS Sports, Sports, Sports   **My Spelling Test**

Find the correct answer. Fill in the circle.

1. In which sentence does the line separate the subject and the predicate?
   ● Torey's coach / took the team to the state finals.
   ○ Torey's / coach took the team to the state finals.
   ○ Torey's coach took / the team to the state finals.

2. In which sentence does the line separate the subject and predicate?
   ○ Michael / soccer last year.
   ● Michael / played soccer last year.
   ○ Michael player soccer / last year.

3. Which word is spelled correctly?
   ○ skatboarde
   ○ skateborde
   ● skateboard

4. Which word means "a situation when two teams have the same score"?
   ● tie
   ○ point
   ○ river

5. Write the sentence correctly.
   our coche told evrybody to play bassketball outside
   Our coach told everybody to play
   basketball outside.

Ask someone to test you on the spelling words.

1. _____
2. _____
3. _____
4. _____
5. _____
6. _____
7. _____
8. _____
9. _____
10. _____

32   ASSESSMENT 3   Spell & Write • EMC 4539 • ©2005 by Evan-Moor Corp.

Page 33

Family Rap

People who love you,
People who share,
They're the ones
Who'll always care.
A family.

People together,
People who say,
"We're proud of you
In every way."
A family.

People who help you,
People who make
A home that's happy.
It's no mistake.
A family.

People who know you,
People who see
All that you are,
And all you can be.
A family.

Find It! Read the spelling words.
Check off the words you can find in the story.

☐ I'm ☑ it's ☑ they're ☑ we're ☐ o'clock
☐ let's ☑ together ☑ home ☑ family ☑ that's

How many spelling words did you find? 7

Page 35

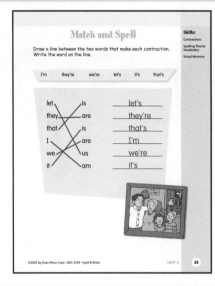

Match and Spell

Skills:
Contractions
Spelling Theme
Vocabulary
Visual Memory

Draw a line between the two words that make each contraction.
Write the word on the line.

I'm they're we're let's it's that's

let · is → let's
they · are → they're
that · is → that's
I · are → I'm
we · us → we're
it · am → it's

Page 36

Skills:
Contractions
Spelling Theme
Vocabulary
Visual Memory

Spell It

Circle the correctly spelled word in each row.

1. were' (we're) wee're
2. hume homme (home)
3. toogeter (together) tugethr
4. (let's) lett's lets'
5. (family) fammile famully
6. thayre they'er (they're)
7. oh'clock (o'clock) o'clocke
8. tha'ts thats' (that's)
9. (I'm) I'am I'me
10. i'ts its' (it's)

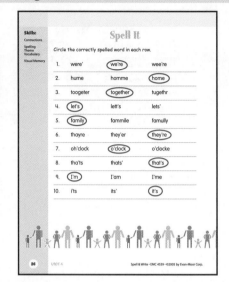

Page 37

Contraction Action

Skills:
Using Apostrophes to Make Contractions

Use an apostrophe (') when making a contraction. The apostrophe takes the place of the missing letter or letters.

let us   let's   I am   I'm

Cross out the letter or letters in each set of words to make a contraction. Replace the letter or letters with an apostrophe. Write the contraction on the line. The first one has been done for you.

1. we w~~ill~~ we'll
2. have n~~o~~t haven't
3. I w~~ill~~ I'll
4. they ~~a~~re they're
5. he ~~i~~s he's
6. it ~~i~~s it's
7. can n~~o~~t can't
8. did n~~o~~t didn't

Page 38

Skills:
Visual Memory
Contractions

Circle It!

Circle the correct spelling.

1. Imer (I'm) going to my soccer game.
2. My famile (family) is coming to watch.
3. The game starts at four (o'clock) oclock.
4. (It's) Its going to be a good game.
5. Weer'e (We're) going out for pizza afterward.
6. They know (that's) thatts my favorite food.

Page 40

Skills:
Writing a Poem

Families Care

Write a poem using the letters in the word family. Think of all the ways your family cares for you. Then write something that starts with each letter in the word. Your poem does not have to rhyme.

Examples:
Feeds and clothes me
Always there for me

F _____ Responses will vary.
A _____
M _____
I _____
L _____
Y _____

Page 41

My Family Is Special

Skills:
Writing a Personal Narrative

What makes your family special? Do you share a special tradition, event, talent, or relative? Write about your family below. Use as many spelling words as you can.

I'm it's they're we're o'clock
let's together home family that's

Responses will vary.

Check Your Writing
☐ I used a capital letter for each name.
☐ I checked my spelling.

Page 42

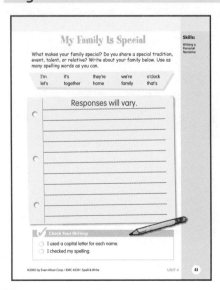

TEST YOUR SKILLS — Family Rap

Find the correct answer. Fill in the circle.

1. Which contraction is made up of the two underlined words?
Jenny does not want to leave her family.
○ don't
● doesn't
○ didn't

2. Which contraction is made up of the two underlined words?
Mando is not ready for his test.
○ won't
○ it's
● isn't

3. Which word is spelled correctly?
○ familiy
● family
○ famly

4. Which word means "a place where you live or belong"?
● home
○ o'clock
○ it's

5. Write the sentence correctly.
letts get tugethr when theyre finished
Let's get together when they're finished.

My Spelling Test

Ask someone to test you on the spelling words.

1. _____
2. _____
3. _____
4. _____
5. _____
6. _____
7. _____
8. _____
9. _____
10. _____

Spell & Write • EMC 4539 • © Evan-Moor Corporation

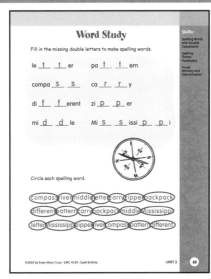

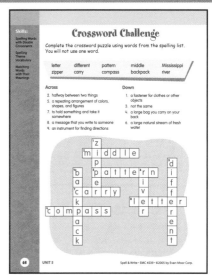

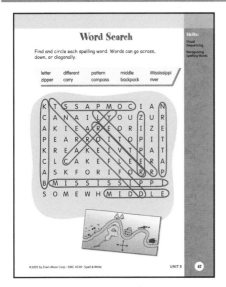

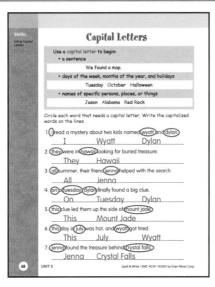

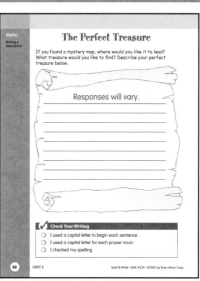

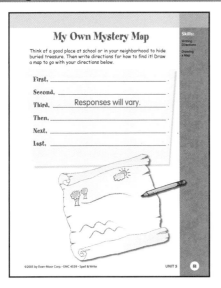

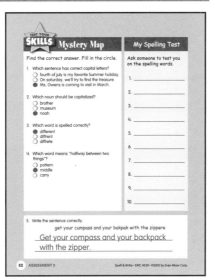

Money Matters

My grandpa is teaching me an important lesson—how to save my money. He has given me fifty dollars for my birthday every year. He takes me to the bank where I have an account. The bank teller puts the money in my account, and she writes the amount in my bankbook. Do you know what the bank does? It pays me for using my money!

Grandpa showed me how to save some money in a change jar, too. I put in quarters, dimes, nickels, and pennies. When the jar is full, I count the money. Then I put it into two piles. I keep one pile to spend, and I take the other to the bank. I like to read my bankbook. I can see my savings grow.

Find It! Read the spelling words. Check off the words you can find in the story.

☐ again ✓ given ✓ other ✓ does ✓ some
✓ money ✓ change ✓ read ✓ bank ✓ save

How many spelling words did you find? 9

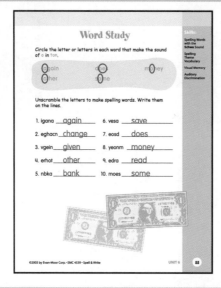

Word Study

Circle the letter or letters in each word that make the sound of o in ton.

(ag)ain d(oe)s m(o)ney
(o)ther (o)ne

Unscramble the letters to make spelling words. Write them on the lines.

1. igana __again__   6. vesa __save__
2. eghacn __change__   7. eosd __does__
3. vgein __given__   8. yeonm __money__
4. erhot __other__   9. edra __read__
5. nbka __bank__   10. moes __some__

Write It Right

Circle the misspelled words. Write them correctly on the lines.

1. Let's take our (munny) to the (banck).
   __money__   __bank__
2. Mom has (givun) me (sum) coins.
   __given__   __some__
3. (Dous) the teller help you make (chanje)?
   __Does__   __change__
4. I can (reade) what I (sav) in my bankbook.
   __read__   __save__
5. My (uther) piggy bank is full (agane).
   __other__   __again__

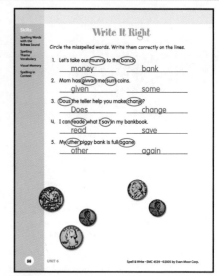

Kinds of Sentences

There are four kinds of sentences. Each kind uses specific ending punctuation.
- A **statement** tells something. It ends with a period. (.)
- A **question** asks something. It ends with a question mark. (?)
- A **command** tells someone to do something. It ends with a period. (.)
- An **exclamation** shows strong feeling. It ends with an exclamation mark. (!)

Add the correct ending punctuation. Then write whether each sentence is a statement, question, command, or exclamation.

1. Did you count all your money **?**   __question__
2. Put your money in the bank **.**   __command__
3. Wow, look at all that money **!**   __exclamation__
4. The bank is behind the library **.**   __statement__
5. Who is the bank teller today **?**   __question__
6. My house is on fire **!**   __exclamation__
7. Did you save enough for a coat **?**   __question__
8. Count this change **.**   __command__

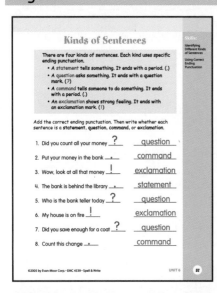

Make a Match

Draw a line from each spelling word to its meaning.

again — one more time
given — to have handed something to another person
other — different, not the same
does — performing an action
some — an amount that is not named
money — coins and bills people use to buy things
change — coins, not bills
read — to look at written words and understand what they mean
bank — a place where people keep their money
save — to keep money to use in the future

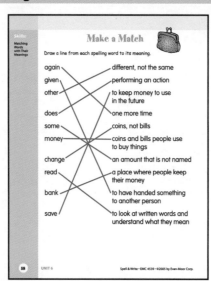

Lots of Money

You just won first place in a contest! You won $10,000! What are you going to do with the money? Buy presents? Save it in the bank? Go on a trip? List ten things you would do with the money.

1. _____
2. ____ Responses will vary. ____
3. _____
4. _____
5. _____
6. _____
7. _____
8. _____
9. _____
10. _____

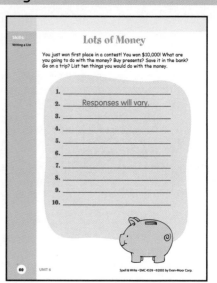

Lost and Found

You've just found a wallet at the park. It's stuffed full of money! What will you do with it? Write your story below. Use as many spelling words as you can.

again given other does some
money change read bank save

_____ Responses will vary. _____

✓ Check Your Writing
☐ I used a capital letter to begin each sentence.
☐ I used correct punctuation at the end of each sentence.
☐ I checked my spelling.

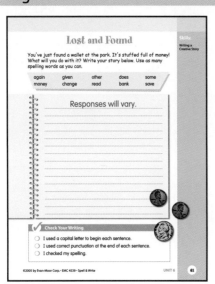

TEST YOUR SKILLS Money Matters   **My Spelling Test**

Find the correct answer. Fill in the circle.   Ask someone to test you on the spelling words.

1. What kind of sentence is this?
   Did you save your money in that jar?
   ○ statement
   ● question
   ○ command
   ○ exclamation

2. What kind of sentence is this?
   Come with me to the bank.
   ○ statement
   ○ question
   ● command
   ○ exclamation

3. Which word is spelled correctly?
   ○ chanje
   ○ chainge
   ● change

4. Which word means "different, not the same as mentioned"?
   ● other
   ○ some
   ○ again

5. Write the sentence correctly.
   they have given me monny to savve in the banck
   __They have given me money to save in__
   __the bank.__

1. _____
2. _____
3. _____
4. _____
5. _____
6. _____
7. _____
8. _____
9. _____
10. _____

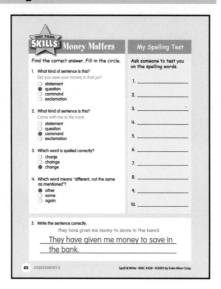

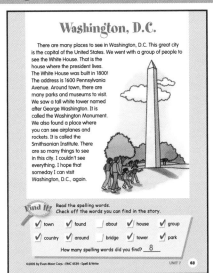

Washington, D.C.

There are many places to see in Washington, D.C. This great city is the capital of the United States. We went with a group of people to see the White House. That is the house where the president lives. The White House was built in 1800! The address is 1600 Pennsylvania Avenue. Around town, there are many parks and museums to visit. We saw a tall white tower named after George Washington. It is called the Washington Monument. We also found a place where you can see airplanes and rockets. It is called the Smithsonian Institute. There are so many things to see in this city. I couldn't see everything. I hope that someday I can visit Washington, D.C., again.

Find It! Read the spelling words. Check off the words you can find in the story.

✓ town ✓ found ☐ about ✓ house ✓ group
✓ country ✓ around ☐ bridge ✓ tower ✓ park

How many spelling words did you find? _8_

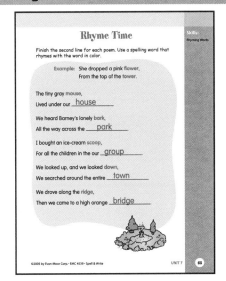

Rhyme Time

Skills: Rhyming Words

Finish the second line for each poem. Use a spelling word that rhymes with the word in color.

Example: She dropped a pink flower,
From the top of the tower.

The tiny gray mouse,
Lived under our _house_

We heard Barney's lonely bark,
All the way across the _park_

I bought an ice-cream scoop,
For all the children in the our _group_

We looked up, and we looked down,
We searched around the entire _town_

We drove along the ridge,
Then we came to a high orange _bridge_

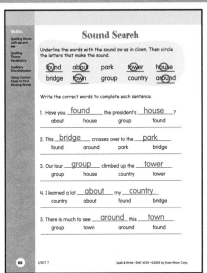

Skills:
Spelling Words with ou and ow
Spelling Theme Vocabulary
Auditory Discrimination
Using Context Clues to Find Missing Words

Sound Search

Underline the words with the sound ow as in clown. Then circle the letters that make the sound.

found   about   park   tower   house
bridge   town   group   country   around

Write the correct words to complete each sentence.

1. Have you _found_ the president's _house_ ?
   about   house   group   found

2. This _bridge_ crosses over to the _park_
   found   around   park   bridge

3. Our tour _group_ climbed up the _tower_
   group   house   country   tower

4. I learned a lot _about_ my _country_
   country   about   found   bridge

5. There is much to see _around_ this _town_
   group   town   around   found

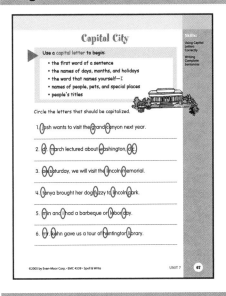

Capital City

Skills:
Using Capital Letters Correctly
Writing Complete Sentences

Use a capital letter to begin:
• the first word of a sentence
• the names of days, months, and holidays
• the word that names yourself—I
• names of people, pets, and special places
• people's titles

Circle the letters that should be capitalized.

1. josh wants to visit the grand canyon next year.

2. dr. march lectured about washington, d.c.

3. on saturday, we will visit the lincoln memorial.

4. tanya brought her dog fuzzy to lincoln park.

5. min and i had a barbeque on labor day.

6. mr. kahn gave us a tour of huntington library.

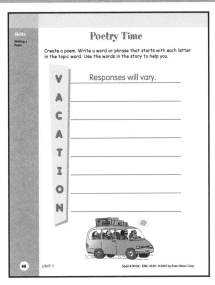

Poetry Time

Skills:
Writing a Poem

Create a poem. Write a word or phrase that starts with each letter in the topic word. Use the words in the story to help you.

V
A
C
A
T
I
O
N

Responses will vary.

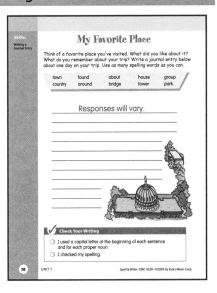

Skills:
Writing a Journal Entry

My Favorite Place

Think of a favorite place you've visited. What did you like about it? What do you remember about your trip? Write a journal entry below about one day on your trip. Use as many spelling words as you can.

town   found   about   house   group
country   around   bridge   tower   park

Responses will vary.

✓ **Check Your Writing**
☐ I used a capital letter at the beginning of each sentence and for each proper noun.
☐ I checked my spelling.

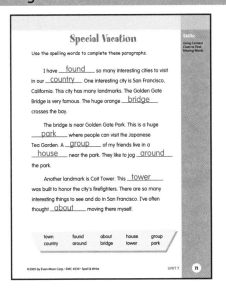

Special Vacation

Skills:
Using Context Clues to Find Missing Words

Use the spelling words to complete these paragraphs.

I have _found_ so many interesting cities to visit in our _country_ . One interesting city is San Francisco, California. This city has many landmarks. The Golden Gate Bridge is very famous. The huge orange _bridge_ crosses the bay.

The bridge is near Golden Gate Park. This is a huge _park_ where people can visit the Japanese Tea Garden. A _group_ of my friends live in a _house_ near the park. They like to jog _around_ the park.

Another landmark is Coit Tower. This _tower_ was built to honor the city's firefighters. There are so many interesting things to see and do in San Francisco. I've often thought _about_ moving there myself.

town   found   about   house   group
country   around   bridge   tower   park

TEST YOUR SKILLS Washington, D.C.   My Spelling Test

Find the correct answer. Fill in the circle.

Ask someone to test you on the spelling words.

1. Which sentence has correct capital letters?
   ● Mrs. Quinn showed us the Boston Museum of Art.
   ○ Mrs. Quinn showed us the boston Museum of art.
   ○ mrs. Quinn showed us the Boston museum of art.

2. Which sentence has correct capital letters?
   ○ jesse and I went to san francisco, california.
   ● Jesse and I went to San Francisco, California.
   ○ Jesse and i went to San Francisco, california.

3. Which word is spelled correctly?
   ● tower
   ○ towur
   ○ touer

4. Which word means "a part of the world with its own borders and government"?
   ○ bridge
   ○ town
   ● country

1. _____
2. _____
3. _____
4. _____
5. _____
6. _____
7. _____
8. _____
9. _____
10. _____

5. Write the sentence correctly.
   our group crossed Lily Bridge on the tour arrownd toun
   Our group crossed Lily Bridge on the tour
   around town.

In the Pond

It's April. It's spring. Time for all the baby animals to come out to play. Quiet! Look over there in the pond. Can you see the ducklings? There are six newborn babies following their mother. The little ducklings are learning how to swim. Mother duck knows how to raise her babies. She shows them where to find delicious duckweed. She also shows them how to dive. Watch those curious ducklings dive among the pond plants. Splash! Splash! A beautiful white swan swims to its nest, and a tiny brown tadpole wiggles to safety. Finally, the baby ducklings waddle home behind their mother. They are going back to their nest. The pond is quiet again.

Find It! Read the spelling words. Check off the words you can find in the story.

☑ April ☑ babies ☑ over ☑ tiny ☑ raise
☑ white ☑ those ☑ duckweed ☑ duckling ☐ tadpole

How many spelling words did you find? 10

Word Search

Find and circle the spelling words in this word search. Words can go across, down, or diagonally.

Skills: Spelling Words with Long a and Long i; Spelling Theme Vocabulary; Visual Memory

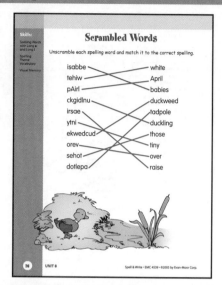

Skills: Spelling Words with Long a and Long i; Spelling Theme Vocabulary; Visual Memory

Scrambled Words

Unscramble each spelling word and match it to the correct spelling.

isabbe — white
tehiw — April
pAirl — babies
ckgidlnu — duckweed
irsae — tadpole
ytni — duckling
ekwedcud — those
orev — tiny
sehot — over
dotlepa — raise

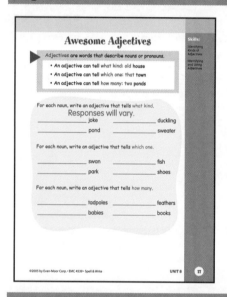

Awesome Adjectives

Skills: Identifying Kinds of Adjectives; Identifying and Using Adjectives

Adjectives are words that describe nouns or pronouns.
• An adjective can tell what kind: old house
• An adjective can tell which one: that town
• An adjective can tell how many: two ponds

For each noun, write an adjective that tells what kind.
Responses will vary.
_____ joke   _____ duckling
_____ pond   _____ sweater

For each noun, write an adjective that tells which one.
_____ swan   _____ fish
_____ park   _____ shoes

For each noun, write an adjective that tells how many.
_____ tadpoles   _____ feathers
_____ babies   _____ books

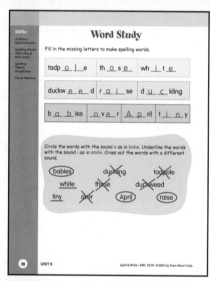

Skills: Auditory Discrimination; Spelling Words with Long a and Long i; Spelling Theme Vocabulary; Visual Memory

Word Study

Fill in the missing letters to make spelling words.

tadp **o l e**   th **o s e**   wh **i t e**

duckw **e e d**   **r a i** se   d **u c** kling

b a b ies   **o v e r**   **A p r i l**   **t i n y**

Circle the words with the sound a as in bake. Underline the words with the sound i as in smile. Cross out the words with a different sound.

(babies)   ~~duckling~~   ~~tadpole~~
white   ~~those~~   duckweed
tiny   ~~over~~   (April)   (raise)

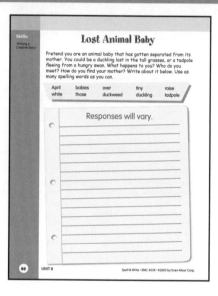

Skills: Writing a Creative Story

Lost Animal Baby

Pretend you are an animal baby that has gotten separated from its mother. You could be a duckling lost in the tall grasses, or a tadpole fleeing from a hungry swan. What happens to you? Who do you meet? How do you find your mother? Write about it below. Use as many spelling words as you can.

April   babies   over   tiny   raise
white   those   duckweed   duckling   tadpole

Responses will vary.

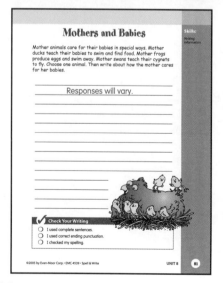

Mothers and Babies

Skills: Writing Information

Mother animals care for their babies in special ways. Mother ducks teach their babies to swim and find food. Mother frogs produce eggs and swim away. Mother swans teach their cygnets to fly. Choose one animal. Then write about how the mother cares for her babies.

Responses will vary.

✓ Check Your Writing
○ I used complete sentences.
○ I used correct ending punctuation.
○ I checked my spelling.

TEST YOUR SKILLS — In the Pond

Find the correct answer. Fill in the circle.

1. Which underlined word is an adjective?
   ● <u>Tiny</u> tadpoles fill the pond.
   ○ We took <u>pictures</u> of the ducklings.
   ○ The ducklings <u>look</u> lost.

2. Which underlined word is an adjective?
   ○ The <u>tadpoles</u> disappeared.
   ● The <u>white</u> swan swam fast.
   ○ The ducklings <u>learned</u> how to swim.

3. Which word is spelled correctly?
   ○ rayse
   ○ raize
   ● raise

4. Which word means "very small"?
   ● tiny
   ○ tadpole
   ○ babies

5. Write the sentence correctly.
   can thoz wite duck babys find the pond
   Can those white duck babies find
   the pond?

My Spelling Test

Ask someone to test you on the spelling words.

1. _____
2. _____
3. _____
4. _____
5. _____
6. _____
7. _____
8. _____
9. _____
10. _____

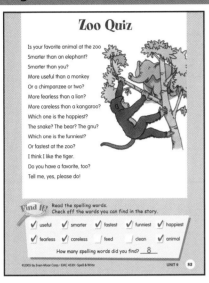

Zoo Quiz

Is your favorite animal at the zoo
Smarter than an elephant?
Smarter than you?
More useful than a monkey
Or a chimpanzee or two?
More fearless than a lion?
More careless than a kangaroo?
Which one is the happiest?
The snake? The bear? The gnu?
Which one is the funniest?
Or fastest at the zoo?
I think I like the tiger.
Do you have a favorite, too?
Tell me, yes, please do!

Find It! Read the spelling words.
Check off the words you can find in the story.

☑ useful   ☑ smarter   ☑ fastest   ☑ funniest   ☑ happiest

☑ fearless   ☑ careless   ☐ feed   ☐ clean   ☑ animal

How many spelling words did you find? 8

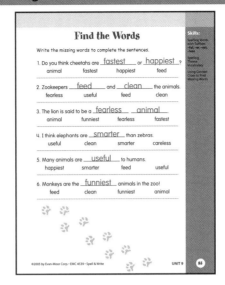

Find the Words

Write the missing words to complete the sentences.

1. Do you think cheetahs are __fastest__ or __happiest__?
   animal   fastest   happiest   feed

2. Zookeepers __feed__ and __clean__ the animals.
   fearless   useful   feed   clean

3. The lion is said to be a __fearless__ __animal__.
   animal   funniest   fearless   fastest

4. I think elephants are __smarter__ than zebras.
   useful   clean   smarter   careless

5. Many animals are __useful__ to humans.
   happiest   smarter   feed   useful

6. Monkeys are the __funniest__ animals in the zoo!
   feed   clean   funniest   animal

Skills:
Spelling Words
with Suffixes
-ful, -er, -est,
-less

Spelling
Theme
Vocabulary

Using Context
Clues to Find
Missing Words

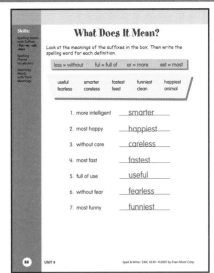

Skills:
Spelling Words
with Suffixes
-ful, -er, -est,
-less

Matching
Words
with Their
Meanings

What Does It Mean?

Look at the meanings of the suffixes in the box. Then write the
spelling word for each definition.

less = without	ful = full of	er = more	est = most

| useful | smarter | fastest | funniest | happiest |
| fearless | careless | feed | clean | animal |

1. more intelligent   __smarter__

2. most happy   __happiest__

3. without care   __careless__

4. most fast   __fastest__

5. full of use   __useful__

6. without fear   __fearless__

7. most funny   __funniest__

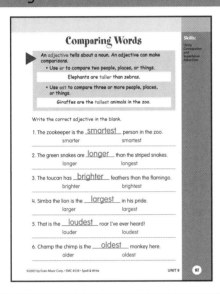

Comparing Words

Skills:
Using
Comparative
and
Superlative
Adjectives

▶ An adjective tells about a noun. An adjective can make
comparisons.
   • Use er to compare two people, places, or things.
      Elephants are taller than zebras.
   • Use est to compare three or more people, places,
     or things.
      Giraffes are the tallest animals in the zoo.

Write the correct adjective in the blank.

1. The zookeeper is the __smartest__ person in the zoo.
   smarter   smartest

2. The green snakes are __longer__ than the striped snakes.
   longer   longest

3. The toucan has __brighter__ feathers than the flamingo.
   brighter   brightest

4. Simba the lion is the __largest__ in his pride.
   larger   largest

5. That is the __loudest__ roar I've ever heard!
   louder   loudest

6. Champ the chimp is the __oldest__ monkey here.
   older   oldest

Skills:
Matching
Words
with Their
Meanings

Make a Match

Write the letter of the definition next to the word.

__e__ 1. useful   a. not paying close attention
__h__ 2. fearless   b. to give food to
__i__ 3. smarter   c. causing the most laughter
__a__ 4. careless   d. free from dirt
__j__ 5. fastest   e. helpful
__b__ 6. feed   f. a living thing that is not a plant
__c__ 7. funniest   g. most cheerful
__d__ 8. clean   h. unafraid
__g__ 9. happiest   i. more intelligent or clever
__f__ 10. animal   j. moving the quickest

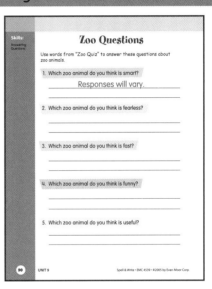

Skills:
Answering
Questions

Zoo Questions

Use words from "Zoo Quiz" to answer these questions about
zoo animals.

1. Which zoo animal do you think is smart?
   Responses will vary.

2. Which zoo animal do you think is fearless?

3. Which zoo animal do you think is fast?

4. Which zoo animal do you think is funny?

5. Which zoo animal do you think is useful?

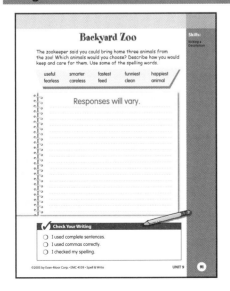

Backyard Zoo

Skills:
Writing a
Description

The zookeeper said you could bring home three animals from
the zoo! Which animals would you choose? Describe how you would
keep and care for them. Use some of the spelling words.

| useful | smarter | fastest | funniest | happiest |
| fearless | careless | feed | clean | animal |

Responses will vary.

✓ Check Your Writing
○ I used complete sentences.
○ I used commas correctly.
○ I checked my spelling.

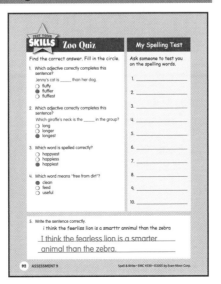

★ **TEST YOUR SKILLS** **Zoo Quiz** | **My Spelling Test** |

Find the correct answer. Fill in the circle.

Ask someone to test you
on the spelling words.

1. Which adjective correctly completes this
   sentence?
   Jenny's cat is ____ than her dog.
   ○ fluffy
   ● fluffier
   ○ fluffiest

2. Which adjective correctly completes this
   sentence?
   Which giraffe's neck is the ____ in the group?
   ○ long
   ○ longer
   ● longest

3. Which word is spelled correctly?
   ○ happyest
   ○ happiess
   ● happiest

4. Which word means "free from dirt"?
   ● clean
   ○ feed
   ○ useful

1. _____
2. _____
3. _____
4. _____
5. _____
6. _____
7. _____
8. _____
9. _____
10. _____

5. Write the sentence correctly.
   i think the feerliss lion is a smarttr annimul than the zebra
   I think the fearless lion is a smarter
   animal than the zebra.

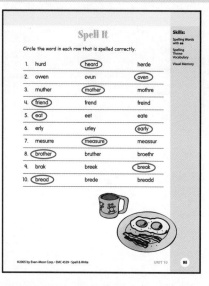

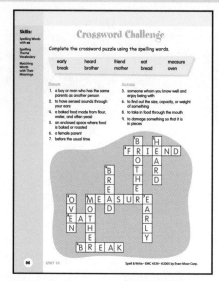

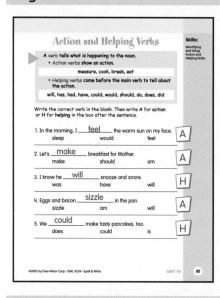

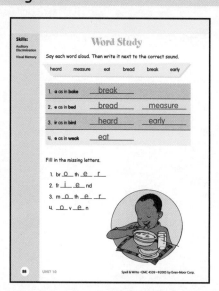

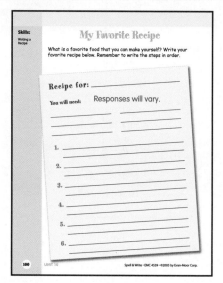

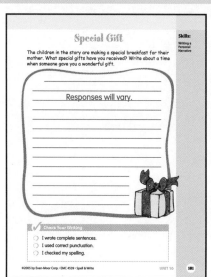

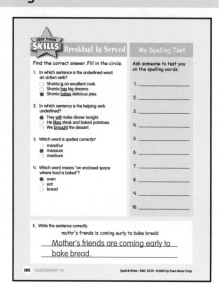

Spell & Write • EMC 4539 • © Evan-Moor Corporation

Page 103

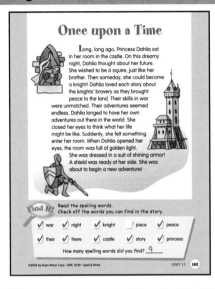

Page 105

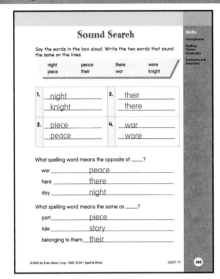

Page 106

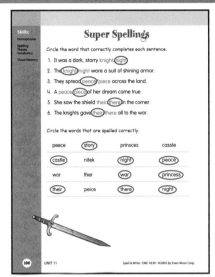

Page 107

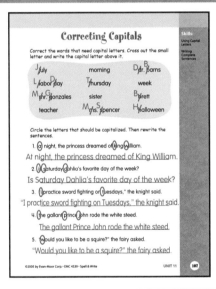

Page 108

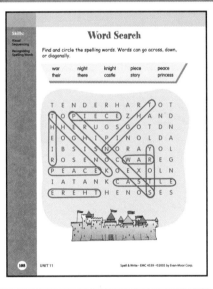

Page 110

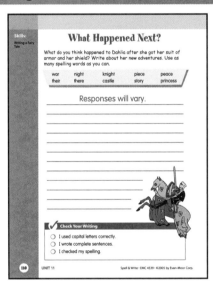

Page 111

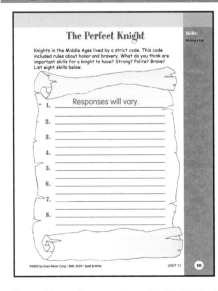

Page 112

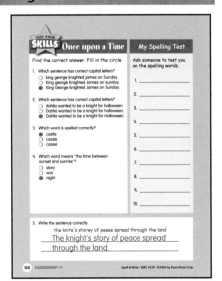

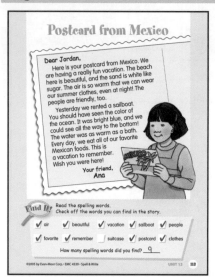

Postcard from Mexico

Dear Jordan,
Here is your postcard from Mexico. We are having a really fun vacation. The beach here is beautiful, and the sand is white like sugar. The air is so warm that we can wear our summer clothes, even at night! The people are friendly, too.
Yesterday we rented a sailboat. You should have seen the color of the ocean. It was bright blue, and we could see all the way to the bottom! The water was as warm as a bath. Every day, we eat all of our favorite Mexican foods. This is a vacation to remember. Wish you were here!

Your friend,
Ana

Find It! Read the spelling words. Check off the words you can find in the story.

| ☑ air | ☑ beautiful | ☑ vacation | ☑ sailboat | ☑ people |
| ☑ favorite | ☑ remember | ☐ suitcase | ☑ postcard | ☑ clothes |

How many spelling words did you find? __9__

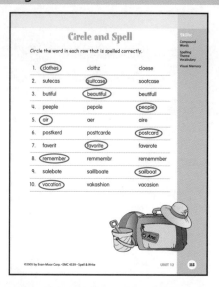

Circle and Spell

Circle the word in each row that is spelled correctly.

1. (clothes)   clothz   cloese
2. sutecas   (suitcase)   sootcase
3. butiful   (beautiful)   beutifull
4. peeple   pepole   (people)
5. (air)   aer   aire
6. postkerd   posttcarde   (postcard)
7. faverit   (favorite)   faverote
8. (remember)   remmembr   rememmber
9. salebote   sailboate   (sailboat)
10. (vacation)   vakashion   vacasion

Skills: Compound Words / Spelling Theme Vocabulary / Visual Memory

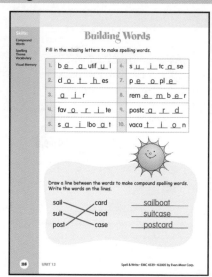

Building Words

Fill in the missing letters to make spelling words.

1. b e a utif u l
2. cl o th es
3. a i r
4. fav o r i te
5. s a i lbo a t
6. s u i tc a se
7. p e o p l e
8. rem e m b e r
9. postc a r d
10. vaca t i o n

Draw a line between the words to make compound spelling words. Write the words on the lines.

sail — boat → sailboat
suit — card → suitcase
post — case → postcard

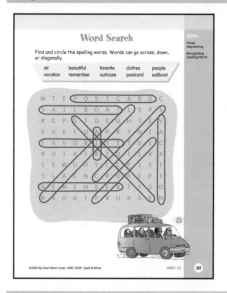

Word Search

Find and circle the spelling words. Words can go across, down, or diagonally.

| air | beautiful | favorite | clothes | people |
| vacation | remember | suitcase | postcard | sailboat |

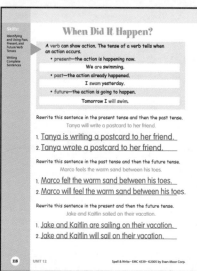

When Did It Happen?

A verb can show action. The tense of a verb tells when an action occurs.
- *present*—the action is happening now.
  We are swimming.
- *past*—the action already happened.
  I swam yesterday.
- *future*—the action is going to happen.
  Tomorrow I will swim.

Rewrite this sentence in the present tense and then the past tense.
Tanya will write a postcard to her friend.

1. Tanya is writing a postcard to her friend.
2. Tanya wrote a postcard to her friend.

Rewrite this sentence in the past tense and then the future tense.
Marco feels the warm sand between his toes.

1. Marco felt the warm sand between his toes.
2. Marco will feel the warm sand between his toes.

Rewrite this sentence in the present and then the future tense.
Jake and Kaitlin sailed on their vacation.

1. Jake and Kaitlin are sailing on their vacation.
2. Jake and Kaitlin will sail on their vacation.

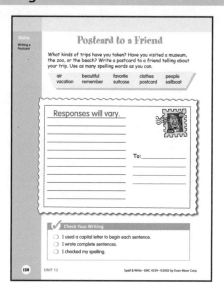

Postcard to a Friend

What kinds of trips have you taken? Have you visited a museum, the zoo, or the beach? Write a postcard to a friend telling about your trip. Use as many spelling words as you can.

| air | beautiful | favorite | clothes | people |
| vacation | remember | suitcase | postcard | sailboat |

Responses will vary.

To:

✓ Check Your Writing
○ I used a capital letter to begin each sentence.
○ I wrote complete sentences.
○ I checked my spelling.

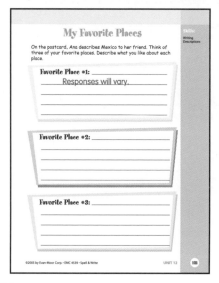

My Favorite Places

On the postcard, Ana describes Mexico to her friend. Think of three of your favorite places. Describe what you like about each place.

Favorite Place #1: _____
Responses will vary.

Favorite Place #2: _____

Favorite Place #3: _____

TEST YOUR SKILLS — Postcard from Mexico | My Spelling Test

Find the correct answer. Fill in the circle.

1. Which tense is the verb in this sentence?
   Jordan will read his postcard after school.
   ○ past
   ○ present
   ● future

2. Which tense is the verb in this sentence?
   Ana travels to Mexico every summer.
   ○ past
   ● present
   ○ future

3. Which word is spelled correctly?
   ● sailboat
   ○ sailbote
   ○ sailboate

4. Which word means "the mixture of gases that surround the Earth"?
   ○ people
   ● air
   ○ beautiful

5. Write the sentence correctly.
   remumbr to bring your fovurit clothz
   Remember to bring your favorite clothes.

Ask someone to test you on the spelling words.

1. _____
2. _____
3. _____
4. _____
5. _____
6. _____
7. _____
8. _____
9. _____
10. _____